Beginner's Prayer

A BEGINNER'S GUIDE TO THE GOSPEL

BY BOB RICE

Designed by David Calavitta

Authored by Bob Rice (with Mark Hart)

Copy editing by Rachel Peñate, Joel Stepanek, and Mark Hart

Copyright ©2015 Life Teen, Inc. All rights reserved.
Published by Life Teen, Inc.
2222 S. Dobson Rd.
Suite 601
Mesa, AZ 85202
LifeTeen.com

Printed in the United States of America.
Printed on acid-free paper.

For more information about Life Teen or to order additional copies, go online to LifeTeen.com or call us at 1-800-809-3902.

TABLE OF CONTENTS

"Maaaaaaaaaaaaarrrrkkkk!" she shouted, letting all in our neighborhood know that my presence was needed at home immediately. I could always tell when my mother was worried about my whereabouts and my mother had the uncanny knack of turning my name – a one-syllable word – into a multi-syllable exclamation that would make even stray dogs flee.

It was in those moments, too, that I lamented my namesake, St. Mark, feeling as though in the large Catholic family lotto for the best saint names I'd somehow lost out. I mean my older brothers could claim devil-slayers like St. Michael, snake charmers like St. Patrick or even St. Francis, animal tamer (and now, ironically, target for birds in countless yards), just to name a few. And then there I was... stuck with good 'ol Mark whose only endearing quality in my young, sarcastic mind was that he wrote the shortest Gospel of the four, meaning that our parochial school Mass should have gone shorter. Alas, my liturgical arithmetic was off a little bit; a shorter Gospel book never meant a shorter Gospel proclamation (or homily, for that matter).

It wasn't until later, during my high school years, that a youth minister opened my eyes to the gift my mother and father had bestowed upon me through their prayerful discernment of my name.

What's in a name?

A closer examination of the New Testament reveals that the author of the second Gospel was actually known as "John Mark" (Acts 12:25; 15:37). Though John was his Hebrew name, he became better known by his Roman name, Mark, and for good reason.

Like the Greeks before them, the Romans had more gods than Cheesecake Factory has entrees. Romans had a god for everything — sex, weather, agriculture, you name it. The Roman god of war was called Mars, of which "Mark" is a derivative. How blessedly different my early childhood would have been if someone would have clued me in on the fact that the name "Mark" – my name – translates to "mighty warrior." That little tidbit would have proven useful on more dodge ball courts than I can count.

Why, though, would the evangelist choose to go by his Roman name as he sought to spread the good news of Christ? Was it because he didn't want to be confused by the far better known "John," the son of Zebedee and beloved disciple of Jesus? The answer actually has roots far deeper.

God designs each of us with a specific mission and Mark was no exception. The core audience St. Mark wrote to were Gentile (non-Jewish) Christians living in Rome. Inspired by the Holy Spirit, Mark's words would bring hope to Christians enduring strong persecution at the time. Given this fact, it should come as no shock that Mark's portrait of Jesus is one of a wonder-working warrior, a perfect combination of divine power and mercy toward humanity. Put simply, if you can "understand" St. Mark's Gospel (which is the shortest and easiest), you will have the foundation to understand the other three and the remainder of the New Testament.

Several things make St. Mark's Gospel quite different than the other three (which you'll no doubt notice on the pages that follow). You won't come across several long sermons in Mark's Gospel (only two, to be exact), nor will you find the "back story" of the nativity that you do in Matthew and Luke. No, in Mark, Jesus is a God of action, performing miracles and casting out demons at every drop of the hat and turn of the page. St. Mark's Gospel is fast-paced and power packed, which is one reason that the symbol associated with St. Mark is the lion. Jesus' power and might are seen on every page... it's as though when Christ speaks, *heaven roars* with love and mercy.

Through St. Mark's pen, the Holy Spirit breathes urgency into every chapter. Should you read the Gospel from start to finish, you'll notice that Mark uses the word "immediately" about 40 times in just 16 short chapters. Note, too, that following the Christ's crucifixion, it is not a Jew, and not even a regular Roman citizen but a high-ranking Roman officer – a Centurion – who first proclaims Christ's identity as the "Son of God" (Mark 15:39). Such a bold statement from a highly trained and revered soldier undoubtedly raised the eyebrows of more than a few in the Roman audience at the time.

Perhaps the passion and the urgency communicated in St. Mark's account reflected as much about the author as they did about his Lord. One must wonder, however, where all this passion and intimate knowledge of Christ came from if St. Mark was not one of the original Twelve Apostles.

The Saints behind the Saint

The New Testament reveals so many interesting things about our early Church, among them that it wasn't much different than the Church today... people didn't always get along.

While Mark was the cousin of St. Barnabas (Colossians 4:10), it was his relationship with two other "VIPs" that gave Mark his credibility and information. St. Mark was a traveling companion to both St. Peter and St. Paul, offering him the best of both apostolic worlds. Peter obviously had a close relationship with the young evangelist, referring to him intimately as "my son Mark" (1 Peter 5:13). Mark's Gospel was obviously heavily influenced by the fisherman turned shepherd, Peter, our first Pope, offering eye witness details that could be known only by Peter, himself (Mark 4:35-38; 5:38-41). In fact, a closer examination of Peter's testimony in Acts 10:36-43 reveals almost an "outline" for Mark's entire Gospel. Whether a scribe or recording secretary or merely a student with pristine memory, Mark's witness to the life of Christ was heavily influenced by Peter's "behind the scenes" eyewitness account.

St. Paul, too, had intimate working knowledge of Mark taking him on his first missionary journey (Acts 13:5) which we come to find out was cut short for some reason, as Mark left the mission early (Acts 13:13). Whatever happened became an obvious source of tension between he and Paul (Acts 15:36-41) but was later reconciled as Mark rejoined him on future missionary efforts (Colossians 4:10; Philemon 24). Paul even publically praises Mark's ministerial usefulness in his letter to Timothy (2 Timothy 4:11).

In Mark we have the portrait of a true disciple, fueled by a passionate love for Christ but still susceptible to moments of spiritual immaturity, self-focus, and stubbornness. He shared the good news (gospel) of Jesus with all he encountered while personally growing in virtue. He didn't wait until he was "perfect" to share Jesus Christ, *Mark sought Christ first, trusting that His grace would fill in the gaps.* The Bible helps us to see where we need to grow in holiness, and offers us invaluable insight into how to do it. That is why Scripture – and books like this one – are so vital to our daily faith walk.

Moving Forward

Are you, like St. Mark, willing to follow Christ wherever He leads you? Are you prepared to use every gift, talent and situation you're given to lead others to Him? Are you ready to encounter *the real Jesus* of the Gospels and not just your pastor's or parents' vision of Him that has been passed along to you?

Praying with Scripture will change your life forever. This little book you now hold in your hands is a true gift, since it will help you get even more out of the Gospel(s) and your Bible, in general. Take your time with this book. Open up to each passage in your own Bible and read it, then read the commentary in this book, then read the passage again, allowing St. Mark (and us) to act as tour guides into the story. Envision the scene. Watch for adjectives. Pay attention to details. Really "enter in" to the moment. Lock eyes with Jesus. See the lion beneath the Lamb's exterior. Allow the

Gospel to inspire and challenge you, to shock and comfort you. Listen closely with the ears of your heart as your heavenly parent calls *you* by name... and be thankful that whatever your name is and whomever you are named after, that by virtue of your baptism you are God's child, and that your name is written in heaven (Luke 10:20).

Happy reading.

St. Mark, pray for us!

WHY SHOULD I
READ THIS BOOK?

Because Jesus is the most awesome, incredible, inspiring, inviting, and exciting person who ever walked the face of the earth. Because the Gospels are the best way to know who He really is and what He is really like. Because something is knocking on the door of your heart to learn more about Him, but you're not sure how to do that.

Come on in. Turn the page. Let me share with you the life of Jesus Christ as told in the Gospel of Mark.

Start Here

The Bible is a pretty big book. Actually, it is more accurate to say that the Bible is a pretty big *collection* of books. Your Bible contains over 70 books (73 to be exact), written over more than one thousand years by forty (plus) different authors, all of whom were inspired by the Holy Spirit. Scripture is the story of how God has revealed Himself to us over history. But, Scripture doesn't exist just to inform us about God, but to *transform* us into His image. Scripture is a love letter from God to you, meant not only to engage your mind but to pierce your soul.

So where do we begin? The Church has an answer: the Gospel of Mark.

I say that because Mark was used for *catechumens*, unbaptized people who were being introduced to the faith. When someone who didn't know anything about God came to the Church and asked about Him, they would tell them about how God became a man who is known to us as *Jesus*. And to learn about Jesus, they would start with the Gospel of Mark.

There are four Gospels that tell us about the life of Jesus: Matthew, Mark, Luke, and John. Of them, Mark is the simplest and shortest. Yet, the Gospel of Mark contains the basic foundation for anyone who wants to have a relationship with Jesus Christ. It is a great place to start reading the Bible. And so, whether you have never read a page of the Bible before, or you are looking to rekindle or strengthen your relationship with the One whom this book is about, the Gospel of Mark is a great place to begin.

> You can welcome catechumens into your parish every year at Easter Vigil. They receive Baptism at this special liturgy aftver several months of preparation through a process called the "Rite of Christian Initiation."

The goal of reading Scripture is to get to know Jesus, and by that we start by erasing stereotypes of who we *think* He is. Many consider Him to be a nice hippie who loved animals, and preached peace and love. Others think He was kind of a hipster who had some nice sayings. Some try to claim that He never existed at all.

As we will read in Mark, all these ideas about Jesus are wrong. Jesus was real, and no one has had the kind of impact on the world as this man did. But He was more than a man; He was (and is) God. God came to earth to dwell among His children, so that by His life He might show us how to live, and by His death we might be freed from sin. It is, as many have called it, "The Greatest Story Ever Told."

> The Gospel of Mark contains the basic foundation for anyone who wants to have a relationship with Jesus Christ. It is a great place to start reading the Bible.

It's not just *a* story, but *your* story. The tale of the One who loves enough to die on a cross is happening *now*, as He speaks to you through the sacred words of Scripture. When you pick up the Bible, what you hold in your hand is God's cell phone. It's how He communicates with you when you're not face to face in His sacraments. It is His *living* Word. These are not "dead," outdated statements that need to be updated or "dusted off" from antiquity. God is speaking to you right here, right now.

Scripture shouldn't just be *read*; it should but *prayed*. It's okay to admit that you don't know how to pray. Praying Scripture means that you come not to just learn about God, but to encounter God. It means you seek not just information for your mind, but transformation of your heart. Similar to how you learn in school; you may understand Science, but that doesn't mean you love or even enjoy the subject. So how do you go from "knowing" God in your head to knowing and trusting God with your heart? Prayer.

Praying Scripture sees the Bible not as something written for *others*, but for *you*. It means you take a deep breath and quiet your mind (and your soul) before you read it. It means you are attentive to every word. It means you don't rush to finish it, as though it were just another task to accomplish. It means that when you hear Scripture speak to you, you would speak back.

This is how you can pray with Scripture:

1. *Always begin by asking God to help you.* Acknowledge before God that you believe this is His Word, and ask (even beg) the Holy Spirit to speak to you through it. Open your heart to hear His voice, and be willing to do what He asks of you.

2. *Still yourself before the Lord.* Take a few moments of quiet before you begin. Reading Scripture isn't like reading a normal book. We need to ask God to guide us, get rid of distractions, read the text, and then listen to God. Our minds are filled with so many distractions: music in our heads, shows we want to watch, homework we need to do, people who have hurt us... it becomes hard to focus on anything. Power off your phone. Turn off any screens in your vicinity. Remove all noise. Next, ask God to remove any other distractions from your mind, so that you can be more present to Him. Think of it this way: If you were going out on a date with someone, but ten of your friends showed up, what would you do? Well, if you really wanted to spend some time with your date, you would ask them to leave. That doesn't mean there isn't time to hang with your friends later, it just means that *now is not the time.* It is the same way with your time of prayer. You might have very important things to think about or problems to solve, but *now is not the time.* They'll be there when you are finished. Right now, spend a few moments of quiet before the Lord, so that you can hear Him speak to you. Who knows? He might give you the very answers to the things that you worry about so much.

> Reading Scripture isn't like reading a normal book. We need to ask God to guide us, get rid of distractions, read the text and then listen to God.

3. *Read Scripture.* Each reflection in this book is preceded by a passage from St. Mark's Gospel. Make time to read the passage. In fact, read it a few times. Use your imagination to make it become more real (this is why God gave you your imagination).

Use your five senses to make it more alive. Imagine what you read from different people's point of view. Do you hear the sound of the sea as Peter walks upon the water? Can you feel the heat of the sun as Jesus preaches to the crowds? Can you taste the bread He broke at the Last Supper?

4. Listen to God. The Holy Spirit often speaks in whispers (which is why it's important that you quiet yourself before you begin). As you read, a phrase or thought might jump out at you. When that happens, take time to reflect upon that — the Spirit is trying to communicate with your heart or inform your mind. Everything in the Gospels relates to our life. Ask God how what you read applies to you. Don't ever read Scripture and think that you've read about someone else. It's about *Him*, and it's about *you*.

That's how you pray Scripture. If you follow these simple steps, the Bible will never be boring to you. It will become an intimate moment with God that you will look forward to every day. Yes, I said "intimate" because intimacy is far more than a "physical" encounter with another. Intimacy actually has far more to do with our souls than with our bodies. The word intimacy comes from a Latin word that means "to make the innermost known." It is during prayer that we share our innermost self – our thoughts, fears, struggles, hopes, and joys – with God and through His Word and His Sacraments that Christ does the same.

By the way, it's important to ask questions as you go. Yes, the Bible was written for you, but it was also written 2,000 years ago, so there are bound to be things that might not make sense right away. Keep a journal with you and write down questions that

> The word intimacy comes from a Latin word that means "to make the innermost known."

you have. We have become a culture that doesn't ask questions, and is more concerned with acting like we know what is going on than really knowing about it. It stops us from knowing God. Don't be afraid to ask questions about what you read in Sacred Scripture. Your parish priest or youth minister are great people that can help answer your questions. Jesus said, "Ask, and it will be given you; seek, and you will find; knock, and it will be opened to you" (Matthew 7:7). To *ask* means we admit that we don't know the answer. To *seek* means we're not sure where to find it. To *knock* means we humble ourselves at the door of God and request His help. You will have to do all three (ask, seek, and knock) if you are to be blessed by Him in this endeavor.

To help you, I've included a simple walk through of the Gospel of Mark. If you do it every day, it should take you about a month or so to do. I've offered my reflections as an example of a way to pray Scripture. *Please*, don't spend more time on my reflections than you do the Gospel. My prayer is that, once you get the hang of it, you'll be so captivated by what God is saying to you directly through Scripture that you'll forget to even read what I wrote. It is your encounter with Christ through Scripture that is the goal here. I pray that the Spirit may inspire these reflections, but, more importantly, I pray that the Spirit will inspire you as you open His Holy Word. I am honored to help you on this journey.

> Don't be afraid to ask questions about what you read in Sacred Scripture. Your parish priest or youth minister are great people that can help answer your questions.

Some tips to get the most out of this book:

- **Do one a day, every day**. Make a decision to commit time each day to read this Gospel. But if you skip a day, don't try to "catch up," just pick up where you left off. The goal isn't to finish on time, but allow Scripture to slowly transform your life. By the end of the month, you *will* have a deeper relationship with Jesus than you do right now.

- **Make it real**. At the end of each reflection is a "Food for Thought" suggestion on how to make what you have read become real in your life. A journal is a great way to reflect on what the Gospel of Mark means, and will become a great thing to look back on as your life in Christ continues to grow. Make sure to take some time with these ideas — they are ways that can bring this Gospel into your life.

- **Keep it in the context of prayer**. You're not reading to learn about history. You are participating in the life of Jesus Christ, who wants you to know more about His love for you, and how you can live His life to the fullest. He is present in the page. So, talk to Him, and let Him talk to you.

Each week I've included a prayer of the Church for you. You can use it before or after each reading and reflection. But just because you start a new week doesn't mean you have to abandon the previous week's prayers — memorize them and say them all the time.

Breaking the Bible Code

Some of you reading this book might be "getting into" the Bible for the first time, and might be confused when you see things like "1 John 2:15" or "Mark 5:10-20." This is the way we navigate through Scripture and find what we are looking for. It always goes like this: *"Book Chapter: Verse."* So, "Mark 5:10-20" means the *book* of Mark, *chapter* 5:*verses* 10-20. Check the index of your Bible to find where the books are (they're not listed in alphabetical order, so you might have to search a bit). Still can't find it? Books with longer names will often have abbreviations (the 1st letter to the Corinthians will be "1 Corinthians" or even "1 Cor"), so see what is closest. Everybody pretty much uses the same abbreviations, so don't worry! You'll get the hang of it.

Do I have the "right kind" of Bible?

The Bible wasn't originally written in English, so it has many translations, most of which say the same thing in different ways. You'll notice, too, that some Bibles have less Old Testament books than "Catholic Bibles." While it's ideal to have the full Catholic version (73 books), you don't necessarily need it right away to begin the Gospel of Mark. Begin reading the version you have and, if needed, look to get another one soon.

As Catholics, there are a few different translations you will be accustomed to hearing. The readings that are read in Mass are from the "New American" translation of the Bible. The Catechism references the "Revised Standard Version-Catholic Edition" (RSV-CE). But there are lots of versions to choose from, and there are some cool "study bibles" that have extra information to get the most out of the Scriptures. The Life Teen Catholic Teen Bible is a great resource if you are looking for a solid Bible to read and study. It has over 128 pages of additional content designed to help you learn how to read Scripture. You can learn more about it at LifeTeen.com.

The only thing I'd encourage you to avoid are translations that are hard for you to understand. Some Bibles are translated with lots of "Thee's" and "Thou's" and other outdated language. There is beauty in some of that, but I'm not sure it's a great place for you to begin.

The Background

John the Baptist had been preaching for years about a person who would come to redeem Israel from her sins. One day, he points to a poor carpenter's son and says, "He is the One!" This man's name is Jesus, but as of yet we don't know much about who He is. As He slowly begins to reveal Himself to the people around Him, allow Him to reveal Himself to you. Imagine you are hearing about Jesus for the first time. Who is this man?

Prayer for the week: *The Our Father*

Our Father, Who is in heaven
Hallowed be Your Name
Your kingdom come
Your will be done
On earth as it is in heaven
Give us this day our daily bread
And forgive us our trespasses
As we forgive those who trespass against us
And lead us not into temptation
But deliver us from evil
Amen.

Mark 1:1-15

Remember: Don't just read it, pray it! (If you skipped the introduction to this book, then I'd encourage you to go back and find out what the difference is.) Put yourself in the story. Use your senses. Can you hear the Jordan River flowing? Can you feel the water rush around you as you are baptized?

The New Testament starts where the Old Testament left off. After hundreds of years of struggles and sins, God promised that a day would come where He would redeem His people. And He said He would send a messenger ahead of Him. That messenger was John the Baptist.

And what did John preach? *Repent.* The word "repent" means to turn around, to face the direction behind you.

Repentance is when we both feel *and express* sorrow or remorse for our wrongdoings. It's not enough just to "feel bad;" we must do something about it. Repentance is like a 180-degree turn from darkness (selfishness) to the Light (God). This was the message John had for the people who were not facing God. *Turn around.* God is right behind you. He's closer than you think.

Sin is in the opposite direction from God. We can't come to God and dive into sin at the same time. It would be like trying to face East and West in the same moment. We fool ourselves if we think we can do it.

The word "Gospel" means "good news."

John told the people to turn around. He not only preached repentance, but *forgiveness.* We do not turn to face an angry God, but a loving one. This is the Gospel He preached. The word "Gospel" means "good news."

2

As Jesus began His ministry, He fulfilled what John preached. John, whose mission it was to prepare the people for Christ, said, "the time is coming." Jesus said, "The time is now." The kingdom of heaven is here. *It's closer than you think.*

Where do we find God? It's a question that has haunted humanity since creation. Mankind has a natural knowledge that there is a God, but our sinfulness has dulled the ability to find Him. So, over the many millennia of our history, we have tried to guess at the answer. Some made their rulers God. Egyptians believed that their Pharaoh was a god. The Romans, too, held their Emperors in a status almost equal to their (many) gods. Others believed that God was nature (Native Americans). Some believe that everybody is God (Mormons and New Age mysticisms), while others think that God can only be found in nothingness (Buddhists). Who is best to answer this question?

It would seem obvious that God is the best one to tell us where He is. When Jesus was baptized, we see the first real revelation of God as Trinity: the voice of the Father, the descending of the Spirit, and the presence of the Son, Jesus. We see in the beginning of the Gospel that Jesus is not just another person coming to be baptized by John in the Jordan. He is the one the world has been waiting for. He is the one who made the world.

> Egyptians believed that their Pharaoh was a god. The Romans, too, held their Emperors in a status almost equal to their (many) gods.

And His directions to find Him are amazingly simple: *Turn around.*

FOOD FOR THOUGHT

In what ways do you try to face East and West at the same time? What do you need to turn away from to truly be with God? The Gospel starts in the same way our life in Christ does: with forgiveness. Take some time to repent of how you've turned away from Him. Be assured that when you turn to Him, He forgives you.

Mark 1:16-34

As you read today's Scripture, imagine it from the point of view of any one of the fishermen He called. What did they see in Jesus that would make them leave everything to follow Him?

When Jesus called the fishermen, he called them with dignity. He didn't say, "Follow me and be my slaves." He said, "I will make you fishers of men." He did not deny the desires of their heart, He promised to take those natural talents and give them supernatural results.

We are created with a purpose. Even if we don't know God, that purpose our hearts were made for can still come forth. God does not suppose to destroy those talents or desires, but to *transform* them into something greater. But, obedience is the first requirement. Before they can become fishers of men, they must first "Follow me." They had to walk away from their old nets before they were given new ones on Pentecost. vIt not only gave them new strength and unleashed their courage but it also sent them forth with a new mission. They sacrificed their lives because they trusted in the one who called them forth.

> At Pentecost, the Holy Spirit came upon the Apostles and disciples in a bold and powerful way (following Jesus' Ascension). It not only gave them new strength and unleashed their courage but it also sent them forth with a new mission.

It is the sin in us that cries out in fear of this calling. We see it in the synagogue: "Have you come to destroy us?" How often do we ask that question as God comes knocking on the door of our lives? Many feel that following God means their lives will be destroyed. They fear they will become unpopular, unliked, and unhappy. Many think that to be like Jesus is probably boring or very lame. But, that is not the kind of person we read about in Scripture.

There was something about Jesus that was astonishing, exciting, and *attractive*. What kind of man could make fishermen drop their nets, teach with authority, cast out demons, and cure the sick? It is no wonder that the whole town came out to see Him. People who paint Jesus as boring or weak are far from the truth. Towns don't gather to see boring people. And fishermen? Back in those days, fishermen had to be large, strong men to lift heavy loads and pull on burdened nets. Fishermen in Galilee were kind of like lumberjacks in North America. These kind of guys would *not* follow a wimp.

> Following God is different than just believing that God exists. It means we become people of action, like Jesus was.

That day, those fishermen went from cleaning their nets to watching miracles. And they were given a hope of being something greater than they ever thought they could be. Jesus did that in their lives, and He can do it in ours, too. But only if we drop our nets, and *follow*.

Following God is different than just believing that God exists. It means we become people of action, like Jesus was. Jesus not only spoke with authority, but He acted with it, too.

Isn't it incredible that God wants us to be with Him? He doesn't say, "Go over there" but "Come, follow me." I think it's a telling mark of the first disciples that they didn't ask where Jesus was going. Maybe that's because they didn't care. For them, the destination wasn't important. All that mattered was getting to know Him.

FOOD FOR THOUGHT

Many times, we are afraid of what God will do in our lives. What are you afraid of? What "nets" are you afraid to let go of to follow Christ? God is not out to destroy our lives, but fulfill them. If you want proof, check out what He says to us in Jeremiah 29:11 (it's in the Old Testament).

Mark 1:35-45

Jesus Christ was fully God and fully man, like us in all ways except sin. He became like us not only to redeem humanity, but also to teach us how to live.

Isn't it interesting that Jesus woke up early to pray? He found a quiet and peaceful place and then spent time in prayer there. Jesus needed time to be with God, His Father, through the Holy Spirit (it's a deep and complex relationship, I know, that's why the Holy Trinity is our deepest mystery). The fact He took time to pray, though, tells us something about who Jesus is.

Jesus never asks us to do anything that He wouldn't (or didn't) do Himself. He's like the coach who works out with his players, or the teacher who studies with his students. Jesus had every right to say, "You guys should pray. *I* don't need to, 'cause I'm God, but make sure *you* do." No, that wasn't the kind of person Jesus was. He was human. He needed sleep. He was extremely busy. He preached for hours, walked for miles, and cured dozens of people each day. Yet, He still got up early in the morning to pray. If *He* needed it, how much more do we?

Leprosy is a disease that still exists today. Leprosy makes your nerves inactive, and then slowly eats away at your flesh.

Prayer helps us put our life into perspective. It was after prayer that Jesus decided to go on to other towns. I'm sure it was tempting to stay where He was and let people come to Him, but His decision to leave tells us something else about this amazing man. He didn't come so that the lost could find Him. He came to seek and save the lost, and give them the message of God's Kingdom. So, He hit the road and went to other towns.

It was on that journey He came across a man who suffered from leprosy. Leprosy is a disease that still exists today. Leprosy makes your nerves inactive, and then slowly eats away at your flesh. People back then who suffered from it were sent away to live in caves. They wore old rags and had to yell, "Unclean!" if anyone came near them, so that people could know to run away.

They were banned from every town and village, and they were not allowed to touch another healthy person again.

People with leprosy looked hideous. They would have lesions all over their body, and often would lose body parts to the disease. One of these people was courageous enough to come before Jesus, and make an incredible statement of faith. The leper didn't doubt Jesus' ability to heal at all. He knew He could, if He wanted to.

Play close attention to how Jesus reacts, because it tells us a lot about who God is. While the rest of the people with Him were probably reacting with disgust, Jesus looked at him with love. He stretched out His hand, and I'm sure this startled the leper. After all, he hadn't been touched by a healthy person since he got his disease.

Jesus touched the leper. Take a moment to ponder that. Jesus could have said, "Be cured!" and then hugged him once he was healed. But Jesus touched him *while he was still a leper.* His perfect hand rested upon sickened flesh. Imagine how that touch must have felt! And then Jesus spoke those healing words: "I am willing. Be clean."

We have a God who is willing to touch us, even in our most disgusting state. A God who is willing to heal us, even though we don't deserve it. A God who doesn't need us to be perfect to come before Him, but wants us to come before Him to be perfected. That is who our God is. That is what we see in Jesus.

FOOD FOR THOUGHT

Don't forget to pray! It's how we feel His touch. Today we hear that Jesus is never disgusted by us. What aspects of your life are you ashamed let God touch?

Mark 2:1-17

Have you ever been to a party where the place was packed? Have you ever seen a house so full, that you couldn't even get into to the door? Have you ever heard of a person so popular that people would rip the roof open to get to him?

This first story we read in Scripture gives us a little insight into how popular Jesus was. When He would speak, people would hang on His every word. This time, there was one person who was literally hanging — from the ceiling. His friends lowered Him down that he might be healed. Jesus looked at the man, and then said something no one expected. He said, "My child, your sins are forgiven."

Here's something you need to start noticing about Jesus: He usually did the unexpected. His statement brought scandal because, as they said to one another, "Only God can forgive sins." They were right, but they didn't yet recognize that this man who stood before them was, in fact, God come to earth. Jesus then physically healed the man as proof of His power. But the more impressive miracle was not that He healed a paralyzed body, but He restored a crippled soul.

Then He did another unexpected thing. He went to a party at a tax collector's house. In those days, tax collectors were considered traitors. When Rome conquered the Jews, the Roman government would make Jews pay a tax to the Emperor. Romans would have other Jews collect money from their own people, and these tax collectors made their own money by adding to that tax and keeping the extra for themselves. As a result, they were shunned from Jewish society, and were considered the lowest of the low.

And Jesus, this prominent holy man, went to a party at one of their houses. I'm sure the crowd there was very different from the house he healed the paralytic at. The first party was probably filled with the most respected people in the town. The second was filled with "tax collectors and sinners." And the people couldn't figure out why Jesus would hang out with them.

They thought that God was only for the holy. But Jesus made it clear. "The healthy do not need a doctor, only the sick." God is for everyone. It doesn't matter what you do, or who you are, or what people think of you. His message is for all of us: turn away from sin and embrace the mercy of God. *Everybody can be holy.*

Levi, the tax collector, heard this message and it changed his life. As we learn in another Gospel (and also from Church history) this Levi would be later known to the world as Matthew. He was chosen by Christ to be one of the Twelve Apostles, preached the Gospel fearlessly after Christ's death, wrote the first Gospel in the New Testament, gave his life for his faith, and is considered one of the great saints of our Church.

Now, if that's what Jesus can do with a Jewish traitor, how much more can He do with you?

FOOD FOR THOUGHT

Clearly, Jesus did not think that there was anyone too "low" for Him to be with. Do you look down on others? Why is it that you do?

By forgiving sin before healing the body, Jesus taught that our relationship with God is more important than the things of this world. Do you live your life this way?

Mark 2:15-3:6

Note: *Make sure to read through to the sixth verse of the third chapter.*

God is for everybody, but not everybody wants God. Today we start to see the rift between Jesus and the Pharisees. The Pharisees were one of the prominent religious groups at the time. They were the most educated in the faith, and considered by all to be the most holy. But their practice of faith often focused on rules and rituals rather than love. The Pharisees believed more in the letter of the law than in the spirit of it. Outward appearances were far more important than the inward posture of their heart(s).

They were fasting; Jesus' disciples were not. Back then, people fasted as a way to punish themselves over their separation from God (especially after they sinned greatly). So Jesus asked, why should they fast while God is with them? He didn't deny the value of fasting, but made clear that there will be a new way, and a new reason, to do it (that's what He was talking about when He said, "New wine into fresh skins!"). As Christians we fast for different reasons: not for the sake of *our* own suffering, but so that we can be united with Christ in *His* suffering. We detach ourselves from worldly things to be more attached to God.

The Pharisees believed in ridiculously strict interpretations of God's law. The third commandment is to keep the Sabbath holy and not work on that day. The Pharisees came up with "guidelines" to help people obey this rule: they told you how far you could walk, what you could and could not do, etc. They took away the point of the command, which was to honor God by your rest, and turned it into a set of binding laws and restrictions. This day of rest became the most difficult day of the week.

The disciples plucked ears of corn as they walked so that they could make a path without devastating the field (other Gospels add that they ate some corn, too). The reason the Pharisees got upset is because they claimed they were "harvesting crops," a huge violation of the Sabbath law. Jesus shot back at them by sharing an Old Testament story of how King David (of David and Goliath fame) did something that was also against their law (eating bread only priests should eat) because he had a greater need.

The Pharisees believed more in the letter of the law than in the spirit of it. Outward appearances were far more important than the inward posture of their heart(s).

So then they looked to trap Him. Would He cure someone on the Sabbath? The very question *angered* Jesus. They cared nothing for the sick man. They only wanted to see if He would break the "law" so that they could persecute Him.

Jesus will later say, "I have come not to abolish them (the Law) but fulfill them" (Matthew 5:17). He doesn't want us to ignore the Ten Commandments. He wants us to live them in the way they were intended. Jesus never asked us to do something just for "the sake of doing it." We *should* fast and honor the Sabbath, but not as an empty action. We do it filled with the love of Christ, so that we can be more like Him.

FOOD FOR THOUGHT

Our Church tells us to fast on Fridays and rest on Sundays. On Fridays we remind ourselves of Jesus' death, and how He turned away from the comforts of the world to embrace suffering for our salvation. We do this by fasting from something simple: texting, TV, Internet, music, soda, etc. We give up a comfort to be reminded of the cross. On Sundays we celebrate His Resurrection! We do this by going to Mass, celebrating the family He's given us, and avoiding labors that deter our worship of God. Make this real in your own life. What can you fast from? How can you make the Sabbath more holy?

Mark 3:7-19

Our Scripture begins with noting how amazingly popular Jesus was becoming. People were coming from all around the country (and other countries) to see Him and hear Him preach. The crowds got so big that He had to get on a boat so that He wouldn't get crushed by the crowds. He was bigger than any rock star, athlete, or movie star that we could imagine, particularly in a time where there was no TV or Internet, and news spread only by word of mouth. People were healed by His touch, and demons were cast out at the sound of His voice.

To help His ministry, He decided to set up a hierarchy. This is where we see Jesus begin to build the foundations of His Church. He called 12 men forward and empowered them with the message, and the ability to cast out demons.

What was the basis of this decision? Did He choose the most qualified? Did He choose the people who had been around longest? Scripture tells us the reason: "He summoned those He wanted." There was no arguing, no comparing, no resumes handed out. He *chose* them because He *wanted* them.

And what were they to do? First, they were to be His companions. How cool is that! Jesus wanted to have people to be intimate with. (And remember, intimacy is spiritual not just physical.) This is the first and foremost call of an apostle: Be with Jesus.

The second was to proclaim the message, and with that came the power to cast out demons. There was no way He could individually answer the thousands of voices that called out to Him, and He knew the importance of meeting people one on one. So He set up the Twelve to speak in

His place. And to keep them safe in this endeavor, He gave them the power to cast out devils so that they could preach the Gospel unhindered.

The same way He called the Apostles is the same way He calls you today. He calls you, not because you deserve it, but because

He *wants* you. This is why He doesn't "fire you" when you fail so much. It was never about your ability. It is about His desire.

Like the Apostles, your first and foremost duty is to be a companion of Christ. True friendship is founded, not on what you do, but who you are. Since He knows everything about you, there's nothing He will "learn" about you that will make Him change His mind. Do you deserve a friend like Him? No, but *He's* the One who calls *us*.

Finally, He wants you to preach His Word. Not *your* word, but His. The best our words can do is change minds, but His words cast out evil and transform hearts. St. Paul would later write, "I am not ashamed of the Gospel: it is the power of God for salvation to everyone who has faith" (Romans 1:16). I know people who get anxious when it comes to speaking about their faith, worried that they might say the wrong thing. Paul tells us to just speak about Jesus, and let Him worry about the outcome.

Jesus called the Apostles, and we still have Apostles today in our Church (our Pope and Bishops). Apostle is a term meaning "one who is sent."

> Apostle is a term meaning "one who is sent." Jesus has many disciples (students) and from those disciples He chose twelve apostles whom He sent forth with a new authority and mission.

Jesus has many disciples (students) and from those disciples he chose twelve apostles whom He sent forth with a new authority and mission. But all of us share in the "apostolic" calling of following Christ. Now re-read the Scripture, imagine yourself on that mountain, and put your name on that list.

FOOD FOR THOUGHT

I know many Christians who can name all the people in their favorite bands, but not the names of the Twelve Apostles. These are our heroes (except for the tragedy of Judas). Learn their names, and ask for their prayers to help you follow Christ!

Mark 3:20-35

Do people think you are crazy for following Christ? Then you're in good company.

There were many who thought Jesus was "out of his mind." I've heard teens share all sorts of things after they commit their lives to Christ. People think they've lost it, or even say they've joined some crazy cult. It's a hard thing to bear. But imagine how Jesus must have felt when he heard that members of His own family said He was crazy. These are the same people He played with as a child, were there at His bar-mitzvah, and would eat with Him on holy feasts. They were childhood friends, people He went to school with. Simply put, these were people that were very close to Him.

The devil is not an imaginary concept. God created an angel named Lucifer, but that angel rebelled against God (angels have free will like humans do). Now, Lucifer is known as the devil, Satan, or Beelzebul (which means, "lord of the flies"). He is the one who reigns in hell, wars against God, and tries to take His children away from Him.

Their statements must have hurt Him, but the scribes pushed Jesus too far. They had the nerve to suggest that Jesus was working with the devil! The devil is not an imaginary concept. God created an angel named Lucifer, but that angel rebelled against God (angels have free will like humans do). Now, Lucifer is known as the devil, Satan, or Beelzebul (which means, "lord of the flies"). He is the one who reigns in hell, wars against God, and tries to take His children away from Him. In the face of such miraculous healings and holy words, they said that He was of the very one whom He came to save humanity from. After telling parables about how foolish that statement was, He said it was an unforgivable sin to blaspheme against the Holy Spirit (to blaspheme is to take something holy and attribute it to evil).

An unforgivable sin? *I thought God can forgive any sin!* He can, but only if He is allowed to work. The reason blasphemy against God is unforgivable is because you shut off the very method by which you can receive His forgiveness. If you say Jesus is of the devil, how can you ever be saved? It's like taking off your life vest because you think it will weigh you down and make you drown. These people looked God in the face and said He was pure evil. Clearly, their hearts were closed to His love.

Surrounded again by a mob of people (so many that Jesus couldn't even eat), Jesus receives word that His family is there. We don't have a good grasp on the word "family" today. Unfortunately, when some of us hear the term "family" it might bring to mind feelings of pain or brokenness or frustration more than anything else. But back then it meant an intimate connection, a life long relationship that nothing could break. And Jesus stunned the crowd when He talked about who His real family is.

It's anybody who does the will of God. *It's you.*

(A quick word about Mary. The shortness of this scene might seem to paint her in a negative light. But notice it says that Jesus' "relations" thought He was crazy, not His mother. Mary showed up when Jesus' extended family and community went to see Him. Notice that Jesus didn't renounce His earthly family, He just expanded it. Though Jesus was what we would call an "only child," families were very close back then, and He grew up with lots of relatives. The word here for "brother" is a loose one, and can be applied to cousins, second cousins, etc.)

FOOD FOR THOUGHT

Are there times you have mocked others for trying to be holy? Have you held yourself back from doing the right thing because you don't want to seem crazy? What do you need to do to be counted among God's family?

The Background

Jesus began His ministry by proclaiming that "the kingdom of God is close at hand." This week, we'll learn more about the kingdom, the King, and the way we can bring it to earth. We become part of the kingdom by belonging to the family of the King, an offer He made at the end of Part 1 (as you might recall) for those who would do His will. This week, let us ask the intercession of Mary, our mother, for her prayers so that we can draw closer to Christ.

Prayer for the week: *The Hail Mary*

Hail Mary, full of grace
The Lord is with you
Blessed are you among women
And blessed is the fruit of your womb, Jesus
Holy Mary, mother of God
Pray for us sinners now and at the hour of our death
Amen.

Make It Real

The letter of James tells us, "You must do what the Word tells you and not just listen to it and deceive yourselves" (James 1:22). Have you tried to fast? Did you pay attention at Mass? Do you know the names of the Twelve? Don't just nod your head at good ideas and then do nothing about it, make the Word become real in your life.

Let me take a moment to explain what Jesus means by this parable. Oh wait… Jesus just did. Never mind.

This moment is really kind of cool, because we get a "backstage" pass to Jesus' ministry. He speaks in one way to the public, but with His disciples He explains the deeper meaning. It is not a coincidence that He begins speaking in parables right after He is accused of being from the devil. In the beginning of His ministry, He spoke clearly and with authority, and it was distorted in the worst possible way. Now, He's taking a different approach. Jesus begins to use parables to communicate truth to His followers while at the same time confusing His enemies. In a sense, He was "speaking in code."

> Jesus begins to use parables to communicate truth to His followers while at the same time confusing His enemies. In a sense, He was "speaking in code."

He will continue to use parables for His followers throughout the rest of Scripture. And He will often use images that the "common" people would understand (like farming) but the Pharisees and scribes wouldn't get. This parable of the sower is a perfect example.

This parable talks about four ways that people respond to His Word, and each way gets increasingly better. The first group doesn't respond to the Word at all because the devil takes it away. The rocky soil has a little bit of growth, but when trouble comes they quickly die. The seed sown among the thorns grows higher still, but it gets choked by worries, the desire for wealth, and other worldly things. But the great growth is found among those who "hear the Word, accept it, and produce a crop."

All four groups hear the Word. But only the last group accepts it completely and, because they do, produce a rich harvest. God speaks His Word to us all the time, and this parable challenges us on how we might receive it. Will I ignore it because my heart is hardened by sin and let the devil take it away? Will I do it, but only until I get persecuted because of it, and then give up? Will I let the worries of this life, or the lure of lust, money, or power choke it to death? Or will I say, "yes" to it in a way that will change my life?

Though the last three groups have growth, the only one that matters is the one that accepts it fully so that it *produces fruit.* As the Apostle James says, "Therefore put away all filthiness and rank growth of wickedness and receive with meekness the implanted Word, which is able to save your souls..." (James 1:21)

FOOD FOR THOUGHT

How do you usually respond to His Word? What can you do to make your heart a fertile field where His Word can grow in you? Where are there rocks or thorns in your life that can stop you growing in Christ?

Mark 4:21-34

The kingdom of God is coming. Jesus shares a few things about it.

First of all, it will not be hidden. Like a lamp on a lamp stand, it will shine for all around to see. *Second*, you're either part of it or you're not part of it. It's like skydiving — you can't do it halfway, you're either in or you're out. There's no straddling the fence, no in-between. That's what Jesus is saying when He says, "For to him who has will more be given; and from him who has not, even what he has will be taken away." *Third*, it will grow under its own power. The man may scatter the seed, but the crop grows itself. All the farmer needs to worry about is to scatter seed and harvest when it's ready. *Finally*, it starts little but it ends up big. Like a mustard seed, it starts as the smallest seed of all but grows into the largest plant.

These parables not only explain how God's kingdom advances on earth, but also how it advances in our own hearts:

> 1) We receive the Word because someone makes it clear to us. It shines out to us like light in the darkness.
> 2) We then make a decision. We say, "yes" and become a deeper part of it.
> 3) This faith begins to grow more and more in our lives. Though it was initiated by someone else (the "man" who scattered the seed), the real growth of it comes from God.
> 4) And what starts as a small simple thing grows to become the most dominant thing in our life.

In the same way, these parables show us how to spread the kingdom of God, too. We live the Gospel message by radiating it, first, in our own lives and homes for all to see. Our Christian lives aren't supposed to be a secret or private thing, but something lived out publicly. The boldness of this kind of life offers no middle ground. It becomes like a magnet to other magnets: it will attract some and repel others. But the coolest image we get is of the seed growing in the field. The man scatters the seed, and then waits as the seed sprouts and grows. We share the Gospel, but we don't change hearts. That's God's work. All we do is share the Word, and be ready when that life is ready to produce a harvest.

How should we do this? The parable of the mustard seed tells us that you don't have to start big to end big. Here's an example of this from my life: when I was in college, I was constantly sharing my faith, involved in prayer meetings, etc. But the most effective thing I did to share the Gospel was that I said grace before every meal. I always made a point to do it, whether I was with Christians or not. I would always ask if it was okay to bless the food we were about to eat (no one ever said "no"), and then I would say something as simple as, "Lord, bless this food and us as your friends." That little, simple thing did more ministry than the "bigger" Christian events I was a part of.

> You are supposed to be different from the world that does not know Jesus. If you're not, then what's the point of following Him?

It's all about being a lamp. You are supposed to shine. There will be those who do not like the brightness, but that doesn't mean you shouldn't be who you are made to be. You are Catholic. You are *supposed* to be different from the world that does not know Jesus. If you're not, then what's the point of following Him?

It's a dark world, and it needs His light. God needs you to shine so that His kingdom will come. Don't worry about how it happens. It grows by itself. You just need to let God's kingdom bear fruit in your life, and then scatter the seed for others.

FOOD FOR THOUGHT

Do you ever do things to hide your "shine"? What little things can you do to share His Gospel? Here's a classic question that gives another way of thinking about it: If being Catholic were a crime, would there be enough evidence in your life to convict you?

The storm must have been fierce if trained fishermen would cry out, "We are lost!" The man must have been powerful if chains could not bind him, and he called himself, "Legion." Here are two instances where we see Jesus accomplish what others could not ever hope to. He calmed the storm. He sent the demons packing.

I imagine Jesus yelling at the storm as an annoyed mother would yell at a disobedient child. He was mad because it woke Him up from His nap. The story is almost comical when you think of the Twelve Apostles bailing water to save their lives, while Jesus was so tired from preaching and healing that He was sleeping in the stern of the ship. After rebuking the weather, which immediately quieted down, He turned and rebuked the disciples (who also immediately quieted down).

Jesus questioned their faith, not because of what they asked for as much as *the way* in which they asked. "Master, do you not care? We are lost!" It is not only a statement of hopelessness, but of blame. *How can He sleep through this?* they must have asked themselves. *Why won't He wake up and help us?* Clearly, it never crossed their mind that this sleeping man had the power to calm storms. They were probably mad that He didn't grab a bucket and help like everyone else. Jesus was sleeping for the same reason we do: He was human and He was tired. And He awoke with the thunder crashing, lightening flashing, water pouring, and 12 angry men blaming Him for the whole mess.

I wonder what would have happened if they asked Him to help before the storm began to roar. For that matter, I wonder what would happen if we let Jesus in on our problems *before* they get to the point where they overwhelm us. Either way, though the storms may rage and the ship grow weak, we will never sink with Jesus on our boat. And when we cry to Him, His words have the power to bring peace in our stormy lives.

It was the same kind of peace that filled the man from Garasenes. It was so powerful that it scared the townspeople, and they wanted Jesus to leave. (Some people are scared of anything supernatural, even if it is for the good.) Do we see Jesus taking pity even on the demons? No longer able to torment the man, they begged to torment the animals. A herd of pigs were on the mountainside. In those times, pigs were considered "unclean" animals, and it was sinful for a Jew to eat or even touch them. Jesus allowed the demons to destroy themselves rather than having to be destroyed by Him.

These accounts represent two kinds of things that can destroy us. The storm comes from the outside; whereas the demons come from the inside. We face harm by things that are done to us as well as things we do ourselves. But even when the result of these things are so overwhelming that they drive us to despair, Jesus

> Even when the result of these things are so overwhelming that they drive us to despair, Jesus shows His awesome power.

shows His awesome power. But notice how He solved both problems. He could have strengthened the boat, or calmed down the man. But in both instances He went right to the source of the problems and rooted them out. That's what makes Him different from anyone else.

That's what makes Him God. And that's how He wants to help you.

FOOD FOR THOUGHT

Do you cry out to God *only* when your boat is at the sinking point? Do you ask for His help, or blame Him for your situation? Where are you in trouble, from the outside or the inside? When will you let Him free you and bring you peace?

How is one able to touch the hem of a garment? How do you "get into position" to do it? It means that you're crawling on the ground. Jesus, surrounded as He usually was by mobs of people, was on His way to perform one healing when He was stopped to do another. Imagine the desperation of this woman, clawing her way through the crowd to the point where she dives and reaches out her hand to touch the fringe of His cloak. Jesus immediately knew what happened. "Who touched me?" He asked.

This confused the disciples. Here He was, mobbed by hundreds if not thousands of people, and He was asking who touched Him. But the woman knew exactly what He meant. She fell at His feet and told the whole story. She was afraid because her sickness made her "unclean," and it was a direct violation of Jewish law for her to touch anybody, let alone crawl through a crowd of people.

But Christ did not condemn. He did not call her forward to blame her, but to let her know that she was saved. And in this action we see deeper into Jesus' heart. Never in the Bible do we see Jesus waving His hands and curing thousands of people at once. He always did it one by one, making personal contact with each sick person. He wanted to do more than end a sickness. He wanted to begin a relationship.

He wanted to call her *daughter*.

As that happened, the news came that another daughter, the daughter of Jairus, had died. Jesus headed straight to the house, saying, "Do not be afraid, only have faith." The mourners mocked Him, but He just kicked them out. And, taking the girl's hand, He spoke and she came back to life (and was so healthy and full of energy that she began to walk around). As seen in other Gospels, Jesus often kept people silent about His major miracles, or else people would have become fixated more on the miracles than the message.

Strangers risked their lives because they believed in Him. But when He went home, the people He grew up with didn't have any faith at all and would not accept Him. The result was, "He could work no miracle there." These three stories tell us about *faith*.

In Scripture, faith is not just intellectual belief but also inspired action. It is gauged, not by how much you think, but how much you do. The greater the action, the greater the faith. And the more we act in faith, the more God responds.

> In Scripture, faith is not just intellectual belief but also inspired action. It is gauged, not by how much you think, but how much you do.

Just as *knowledge* and *practice* make our faith alive, *doubt* and *fear* make it ineffective. Jesus could cure no one where they did not believe in Him, and was almost not invited to the house of Jairus until He told him, "Do not be afraid."

We are saved by faith. St. Paul later writes, "If you confess with your lips that Jesus is Lord and believe in your heart that God raised Him from the dead, you will be saved." Note that he didn't just leave it at "believe in your heart." He's talking about *knowledge* and *practice*. But be clear that it is not actions themselves that save us — just as touching a piece of cloth wouldn't normally cure a serious illness. It is action inspired by our belief, and transformed by His grace.

FOOD FOR THOUGHT

How can you put what you believe into action? Which stops you from living in faith more, doubt or fear? Pray for the *wisdom* and *courage* you need to follow Christ.

Mark 6:7-29

Today we read not so much about Jesus, but about the ones who followed Him. Jesus sends out the Twelve, two by two, to preach the word, cast out demons, and cure the sick. These were ordinary men: fishermen, tax collectors, tradesmen. But now they are performing miracles! But we also learn about another follower of Jesus: John the Baptist. He was martyred because he preached the truth.

> Sharing the message of Christ is called "evangelization."

History tells us that of the original apostles, one took his own life (Judas), one died of old age (John), and the rest were killed for their faith. Think about that for a second. They gave everything. They offered their very *lives* for the faith. You don't do that for an idea. You don't do that for a set of rules. You give your life for a person, not a premise. They found something so worth living for that they were willing to die for it.

In the creed, one word we use to describe our Church is "Apostolic." That means that the Catholic Church came down to us from the Apostles. Jesus never wrote a book about Himself. He trusted His followers to spread the word. He still does today.

> It's important that we don't be try to fly solo in witnessing our faith — we're not meant to do it alone; there is strength in numbers.

Jesus is commissioning *you* to spread His message. Sharing the message of Christ is called "evangelization." Like the Apostles, we are all just ordinary people. But whoever He calls, He also equips. And the instructions He gave the Twelve are for us as well:

"He sent them out two by two" –

- It's important that we don't be try to fly solo in witnessing our faith — we're not meant to do it alone; there is strength in numbers. Fellowship not only gives us more courage, but it makes our preaching more effective. If one person told you a movie was good, you might believe them. If two did, you'd be more certain to check it out. The more people to witness, the more effective it is.

"Giving them authority over unclean spirits" —

- You do not speak on your own behalf, you are speaking about God. Jesus has triumphed over the devil, and there is not one person who doesn't need to hear about His awesome love. No matter how deeply that person is rooted in sin, the words you share can set them free. Never write someone off from accepting Christ. Don't be afraid of the devil, but stand firm with Jesus.

"Take nothing for the journey" —

- Except for the bare minimum: sandals, a staff, and only one tunic. This is crucial because Jesus tells us that we should be dependent upon Him and others. We don't preach with the attitude, "I have everything and you have nothing." We share our brokenness. We share our humanity. It means we humble ourselves before God and others, but in doing so provide an opportunity for a relationship to begin. By "taking nothing," we are forced to completely rely on God every step of the way. And that's when He can work best in us.

"If you enter a house, stay there" —

- Staying at a house is about building a relationship with the one who lives there. And that's what we must do to spread the Gospel. Sharing our faith is not about having all the right comebacks in an argument. It's about sharing ourselves with others, so that they might see by our life what it means to follow Him.

But make no mistake: doing this will make you a dangerous person to the world. It will kill you in many ways for proclaiming His truth. But Jesus was not afraid to die for us. So, do not be afraid! Our God has even overcome death itself.

FOOD FOR THOUGHT

What can you do to proclaim the Gospel? Who can you proclaim it with? What people in your life would be good to have as a partner to stand beside you, to hold you accountable, and give you the strength to proclaim the truth others might not want to hear? And who do you want to witness to, so that they can get to know Jesus Christ? Who in your life needs what only Jesus can offer? First, find a friend you can evangelize with and, next, make a plan who you will share God with.

Mark 6:30-56

Here we see the humanity and the divinity of Jesus in action. What began by trying to find a lonely place to get some rest turned into one of the largest crowds described in Scripture. "Five thousand men" wasn't just 5,000 guys. The Jews used to count by heads of household, not including women, children, servants, or slaves. Five thousand men could have easily been 20 to 30 thousand people. I think it would have been understandable if Jesus said, "Could you please give me a break? I'm tired, hungry, and I just found out my cousin (John the Baptist) died. Leave me alone!" But instead, He was filled with compassion, and began to teach "at some length."

The Apostles had just come back from preaching, curing, and casting out demons. But even with all these amazing miracles, they were still shocked when Jesus told them to feed the crowd themselves. Their first thought was how much money it would cost. But Jesus didn't want them to gather money; He just wanted them to give Him whatever they had. He took the five loaves and two fish and blessed them. The disciples distributed them, and it fed the thousands with extra to spare.

Something we learn about Jesus here is that He loves to take natural things and make them supernatural events. He could have waved His hand and made everyone's hunger go away, but instead He chose to do it with bread. When people ran to Him to be cured He could have done it from a distance, but instead wanted to touch each one, even if it was only with His cloak. When He wanted to cross the lake, He could have chosen to magically appear on the other side, but He instead decided to take a walk.

The "Feeding of the 5,000" is one of the only miracle stories found in all four Gospels. The other miracle story common to all the Gospels is the Resurrection of Jesus.

This freaked the disciples out. They probably thought it was a demon they cast out that was coming back to get them. It's interesting that Scripture notes Jesus wasn't intending to stop until He realized they were frightened. I don't blame Him, I'd much rather walk on water than be in a boat. There's something beautiful about the God who created the Universe taking a stroll on top of the water in the middle of the night, walking under the stars and the moon He made. Christ invited Peter on the water with Him, and Peter walked on water, too — until he got scared and fell into the sea, only to be caught by Jesus.

Jesus called Peter out onto the water, because He knew that Peter could do it. Jesus asked the Apostles to feed the thousands, because He knew that it was possible. All they needed was faith, and He would take care of the rest. As the Apostles handed over what little they had, so also does Jesus ask us to hand over what we have to Him. It's not enough, but it doesn't have to be. That's the whole point. Too many times we try to do God's work by our own strength. What if the Apostles tried to feed everyone with their five loaves of bread? They would have either given up or burned themselves out. But God never calls us to something we can't do through His power.

When God calls, He also equips. I don't know what great works He is calling you to do, but I do know two things about it: *first*, it is beyond your power to accomplish, and *second*, nothing is impossible with God. When we completely hand over our "natural" things, whether they are talents or possessions, He gives them "supernatural" results.

FOOD FOR THOUGHT

When Jesus got on the boat, He said, "Don't be afraid!" What things are you "afraid" you can't do that God is calling you to? Meditate on and memorize Philippians 4:13.

Mark 7:1-23

For the Pharisees, pleasing God was a matter of the hand, not the heart. It relied on what you did, not who you loved. It wasn't about *being* holy, but *acting* holy. And sometimes, they even used their "holy actions" to oppose God's will.

We still have such Pharisees among us. What does it mean to follow Jesus Christ? For some, it's "do this" and "don't do that." And many go through the empty actions of it, because they think that's what following God is all about. I was once in an argument with a man about something the Church taught, and he responded to me, "I've been a faithful Catholic all my life... I've never missed a Mass on Sunday." He went on to disagree with about every moral precept that the Church taught as true, but in his mind he was following God because he showed up at Church once a week.

It is easy for us to hinge our spirituality on actions we do, because that makes us feel safe. It's easier for us to ask, "God, what do you want me to do?" than "God, who do you want me to be?" But when we truly encounter God, we start to change. We say with Scripture, "You are the potter, I am the clay" (Isaiah 64:7). When the potter applies His hand to the clay, it changes its form. It goes from a shapeless piece of mud to a work of art.

As we experience the love of the Trinity, we find we are melted by the fire of the Holy Spirit, shaped by the touch of the Father, and molded into the image of Jesus Christ.

> There was nothing fake about the way Jesus lived. He didn't come to build Christian robots who all participate in the same maneuvers. He came to save souls and transform hearts.

Our goal in prayer is to always be that melted piece of clay that God can shape. Sometimes, we become rigid in our lives and think we're fine the way we are. That's when we start focusing on how we act rather than on how God loves us. In my years of ministry, I've met kids who on the outside seem perfect, but on the inside have no love. They don't drink, don't smoke, don't have sex, but that becomes the beginning and the end of their faith experience. They think "I'm a good kid" or "I don't really sin" and, in the end, think they don't need God in their life. They go through the motions, but miss out on the incredible relationship that would naturally bear such fruit in their lives.

Jesus is asking that our actions be *real*. There was nothing fake about the way Jesus lived. He didn't come to build Christian robots who all participate in the same maneuvers. *He came to save souls and transform hearts.* Some take these words of Jesus and apply them to another extreme. They think all ritual is bad, and actions have nothing to do with our relationship with Christ.

But nowhere in Scripture do we hear of Jesus missing Temple on the Sabbath, or saying that we don't have to follow the Ten Commandments. He's not telling us to walk away from these things; He's telling us that we can't rely on empty actions to define our faith. We need to do them with our heart. We need to make them *real*. An apple tree doesn't worry about the kind of fruit it makes. It only worries about digging it's roots in the soil to get nourishment. When the roots are established, the fruit comes naturally.

Just because you go to Church on Sundays doesn't mean you're a Catholic. I mean, I could sit in my garage all day, but that wouldn't make me a car. It's not what you do, but who you love and how you love Him. It doesn't mean you shouldn't go to Mass or do holy things, because you should. But when you do, let them be "rooted" in the love of Jesus Christ. That is when they bear the fruit of eternal life.

FOOD FOR THOUGHT

Within what aspects of the faith are you just going through the motions? How can you make them a true expression of your heart?

PART THREE

THE UNEXPECTED CHRIST

The Background

Jesus asked His disciples, "Who do you say that I am?" This week we see more and more of how Jesus is not only fully man, but also fully God. And as the Author of Life, He shares a radical way on how to live it.

St. Francis of Assisi is one of the Church's most well known saints, and he wrote this beautiful prayer that compliments this week's readings.

Prayer for the week: *The Prayer of St. Francis*

Lord, make me an instrument of Your peace.
Where there is hatred, let me sow love;
Where there is injury, pardon;
Where there is doubt, faith;
Where there is despair, hope;
Where there is darkness, light;
Where there is sadness, joy.

O divine Master, grant that I may not so much seek
To be consoled as to console,
To be understood as to understand,
To be loved as to love;
For it is in giving that we receive;
It is in pardoning that we are pardoned;
And it is in dying that we are born to eternal life.
Amen

Keep it up!

If you've made it this far, then chances are real good that you'll make it to the end! Keep making the Gospel of Mark a prayer, and continue to use your imagination to bring it more to life.

Mark 7:24-8:10

In this passage from Mark's Gospel, we actually have three stories, each with particular significance because they happen outside "Jewish territory." In our Gospel so far, Jesus had been preaching and healing only Jewish people. In these verses, however, we see Jesus leave that territory to get away from the crowds that constantly surround Him. But we then see that even among pagan, non-Jewish people, Jesus' reputation had spread. He was recognized even in the areas where Jews refused to live.

> Jesus was Jewish. He wasn't the blond-haired, blue-eyed American hunk that many in our culture draw Him to be. He was a man of Middle-Eastern descent, with dark hair and olive skin.

The Jews had a long and negative history with their neighbors, and since being conquered by the Romans, the Jews had been mocked by other peoples. Scripture goes out of its way to tell us that the woman who falls at Jesus feet was not Jewish, but Syro-Phoenician (a non-believer). We don't know much more about her, except that clearly Jesus is trying to teach her a lesson about the importance and special role of the Jews in God's plan of salvation for the world. In the fullness of His humanity, Jesus was Jewish. He wasn't the blond-haired, blue-eyed American hunk that many in our culture draw Him to be. He was a man of Middle-Eastern descent, with dark hair and olive skin.

That's a surprising image for many of us, and it's why this passage can be so confusing, because in it we encounter *Jesus the Jew*. He is proud of His heritage, and is standing up for it in front of a person who has probably mocked it or looked down upon it. *The children* that Jesus talks about are the Jews.

The "*little dogs*" or "*puppies*" are the Gentiles. "Gentiles" refers to people of non-Jewish belief or descent. Gentiles and Jews did not get along and normally did not interact publicly or privately. The woman acknowledges this fact, but mentions that even puppies get food from the children. And because of her humility, her child is cured.

"Gentiles" refers to people of non-Jewish belief or descent. Gentiles and Jews did not get along and normally did not interact publicly or privately.

She had to humble herself, not only to Jesus, but to the entire Jewish people by recognizing them as the "children:" the instrument through which God has come into the world. We must do the same. The story of the Bible is really about the Jews; we who are not Jewish only get invited to the party at the end of it. Before Jesus, most cultures only worshipped their own cultural gods. The Egyptians prayed to numerous gods (Ra, Isis, etc.); the Greeks did, too (Zeus, Apollos, Athena, etc.).

But it was the God of the Jews that turned out to be the only True God. This is what Jesus reveals to the Syro-Phoenician woman, and later to the rest of the world. This even surprised many Jews, who thought that when God said, "I am the Lord and there is no other," He meant that *the Jews* should have no other god, but didn't think other cultures were included in God's invitation to know and follow Him. Jesus continues His ministry by healing another non-Jew by spitting in his ears. It goes to show that you can never expect how God is going to do His work. And at the end

The Egyptians prayed to numerous gods (Ra, Isis, etc.); the Greeks did, too (Zeus, Apollos, Athena, etc.).

of His travels through that area, a crowd almost as large as the Jewish crowd comes to hear Him preach. And He performs the same miracle with them as He did with the Jews to show that they are now His followers, too (and equally worthy of the same miracles).

Jesus tells us, "Salvation comes from the Jews" (John 4:22). It is because of how God revealed Himself through the Jews that we can know Him and be saved. We who are non-Jewish are now *adopted* children, and that is why the Bible isn't the story of *other* people, but *our* people. God revealed Himself through the Jews, and made Himself manifest throughout their history. Now, everyone is invited to be part of the family.

FOOD FOR THOUGHT

The Jews thought that God was *their* God, but other people had their own and didn't need Him. Do you think that your faith is only for you? How can you share it with others?

Mark 8:11-30

Like all of us, Jesus had good days and bad days. In today's reading, we hear about one of the bad ones. He finishes great ministry with the Gentiles, and then returns to be back with His own people. But who is waiting at the dock? The Pharisees.

They *demand* a sign from heaven. I bet even the disciples thought that He would give them one, just something to show them who's boss. But to everyone's surprise (and disappointment), Jesus just sighed and said, "No." He didn't even stay there; He just got back in the boat and headed towards the other side of the lake.

Back on the boat again, Jesus tried to warn the disciples about the "yeast" of the Pharisees and of Herod (the Jewish ruler at the time). In baking, a little bit of yeast will dramatically change what you are making, taking it from something small and flat and helping it grow to something large and substantial. But the disciples thought He said this because they didn't bring any bread.

Jesus responded, *How can you think I'm talking about bread?* He was stunned at their stupidity. Weren't they there when He fed thousands and thousands of people? Why would He possibly care if they brought bread or not? *Do you still not realize?* The disciples said nothing.

They land at a different town, and people bring a blind man before Jesus, and *they* ask Jesus to heal him. They clearly weren't family and probably weren't even friends. They heard Jesus was coming and grabbed a blind man to see a miracle. So Jesus took the man outside of the village to cure him. Jesus had no problem healing people or performing miracles, but He had no interest in "putting on a show" like some kind of circus freak. That's what the Pharisees wanted Him to do.

He healed the blind man, but in an unusual way. It wasn't an immediate cure, but a slow one. In this, Jesus teaches us about how He heals. It's not always instantaneous. Sometimes, things take time.

The running joke of the Gospels is that the more Jesus told people not to tell others about His miracles, the more they would. That might seem odd, but it also tells us something about who Jesus is. He didn't want to be a freak show or a "miracle worker." He wanted to be a person with a life-changing message. He knew there was a crowd who was waiting to see what happened, so He tells the (formerly) blind man: *Look, just don't even go back to the village, okay?*

Everywhere He went, it seemed that people didn't want to hear Him speak, but wanted to see Him do "magic." Clearly, this was on His mind, and it made Him ask the disciples, "Who do people say that I am?" They mentioned the names of prophets gone before Him. They performed famous miracles, too. But Jesus was so much more than anyone gone before Him. *Surely*, He thought, *my disciples must be able to see that.* So, He turned to them and asked, "But what about *you*? Who do *you* say that I am?"

The silence was broken by the daring voice of Peter: "You are the Christ." Peter was starting to see beyond the miracles. He was starting to get what Jesus was really about.

Maybe it wasn't such a bad day after all.

FOOD FOR THOUGHT

Do we demand immediate results like the Pharisees, or are we willing to let Jesus heal us slowly like the deaf man? Do we get caught up in the miracles and lose sight of the Man? Spend some extra time today praising God, just for who He is.

Mark 8:27-9:1

Peter claims that Jesus is the Christ (yes, I had you read that section again). The word "Christ" means "anointed one." The Israelites had been waiting for Christ to come to fulfill the prophecies made in the Old Testament. It was said that the great prophet Elijah would appear before him and prepare the people for this man who would restore righteousness to God's people. So, the average Jew thought that Elijah would appear with huge fanfare and great miracles, and the Christ would appear after him like a king who would rescue his people from slavery and restore the greatness to the kingdom of Israel. Needless to say, they never expected Christ to be the son of a poor carpenter. It was quite a bold statement of Peter to say that Jesus was the Christ. Peter was right, but clearly he didn't know what "Christ" really meant.

> The word "Christ" means "anointed one." The Israelites had been waiting for Christ to come to fulfill the prophecies made in the Old Testament.

We can see that in the way Peter talks after Jesus shares what will happen to Him. Jesus tells His followers plainly that He will suffer, be rejected, killed, and, three days later, rise again. This news floored the disciples, and particularly Peter. The king rejected? The Christ killed? *That doesn't sound right*, they thought. So Peter tells Jesus that He must be wrong.

Jesus recognizes the voice of the devil behind Peter's words. The devil tells us that the ultimate good is to live a pain-free life of comfort, and we should do whatever it takes to make that happen. There are many today who try to use religion like aspirin, using it occasionally and hoping that it will make the pain go away. All pain is bad, the devil tells us, and all pleasure is good. By this reasoning, any kind of suffering must be wrong, and therefore Jesus shouldn't suffer at all.

That is the way that humans think, because we are creatures of the world. If the only thing that mattered was what happened in this life, then that would be right. But there is something more important than the world, says Jesus. God invites us to be a part of eternity. What good would it do to gain the world but lose your soul? Jesus makes it clear that He is heading in a different direction than the rest of humanity, who lives only for their own pleasure.

We are told that the follower of Jesus must, "take up his cross." This is amazing language! We are used to that phrase because we know of the crucifixion, but think about how strange that phrase must have been to the Apostles. It would be like someone saying we must "be strapped into our electric chair" or "given a lethal injection" to follow God.

Following Jesus will bring you a lot of trouble in this life, no doubt about it. If you are following Him for your own benefit (*to save your life*), it won't work. But if you are following Him to serve Him (*to lose your life*), then you will find a life more abundant than anything you could ever imagine.

It's not like we just suffer now and get to go to heaven later. Yes, we carry our cross, but we can also experience the kingdom of God today. Jesus didn't say that Peter *was* the devil (otherwise He'd kick him off of the Twelve), but He rebuked the demon that Peter was listening to. And he made it clear that the real way to *live* our lives is to *give* our lives. Death is the worst the world can do. But the Christ will rise again.

FOOD FOR THOUGHT

Jesus tells us that suffering is a part of our faith and a part of our life. The devil wants to make us think it shouldn't happen. Who do you listen to? What cross must you carry?

Mark 9:2-29

Don't read those first eight verses too quickly! Take some time to try to imagine what Peter, James, and John saw... They witnessed something more spectacular than any movie special effects could recreate. Jesus appeared in clothes "whiter than white." Moses and Elijah, two of the greatest figures in Jewish faith, stood and talked with Him. The cloud hung over them. The voice of the Father spoke.

They were dumbfounded. They were scared. They had never seen anything like this. Peter suggested they build a tent and stay there. Even though his idea was kind of foolish, I think we can all understand his intent. When we have great experiences with God, don't we want them to last forever? When we go away on a great retreat or a pilgrimage, doesn't a part of us want to "build a tent" and never leave?

We don't know how long this went on, but like all things in life it came to an end. They had experienced some amazing things with Jesus, but this topped them all. They had read stories about Moses and Elijah since they were children, and they just saw them in person! Not only that, but *they* were talking to *Jesus*.

On the way down from the mountain, they asked about Elijah and when or if he would come. Jesus said that he already did. He was talking about John the Baptist. Once again, God did something in a way nobody expected. John the Baptist fulfilled the *role* of Elijah, while people thought that it would be Elijah himself that would return.

They leave the peace of the mountain and enter the commotion of the crowds. The disciples are trying to cast a demon out of a boy, but they can't. The disciples' lack of faith, as well as the father's, frustrated Jesus. But when confronted, the father's lack of faith turned into a statement of hope: *Lord, I believe! Help my unbelief!*

I think this is one of the most honest prayers we hear in Scripture. It is made in complete honesty and humility. It is the desperate cry of a father for his child. Yes, he has faith. Yes, he needs *more*. And Jesus responds by freeing the child from the demon.

> You can't hide your faithlessness anymore than Jesus could hide His glory. But the glory that was Christ can also be ours, if we persevere in prayer and continually say "yes" to Him in our lives.

Why couldn't the disciples cure this child, when they had cast out numerous demons before? The answer was simple: prayer and fasting. You can't always expect to just wave your hand and make the devil go away. You need to be constantly praying, constantly fasting. You need to be spiritually "in shape" if you are going to fight such foes. You must have the kind of faith that goes beyond intellectual belief but results in daily practice.

The bottom line: you can't fake it. You can't hide your faithlessness anymore than Jesus could hide His glory. But the glory that was Christ can also be ours, if we persevere in prayer and continually say "yes" to Him in our lives.

In our readings today we see a mountaintop of faith and a valley of disbelief. We walk through both in our journey with Christ. But through it all, our God calls us to live lives of prayer, and to boldly follow Him wherever we are.

FOOD FOR THOUGHT

You are more than midway through this Gospel right now. Are you still running strong? The father said, "*if* you can heal him, please do." It's like he wimped out, and didn't want to put too much pressure on Jesus or His followers. As we are midway through this journey, ask God to increase your *faith*: not just what you think in your mind, but how you act in your life. Don't be a wimp! Stay vigilant in your prayer times! Be bold!

Mark 9:30-50

Things are starting to change in the life of Jesus. Let's recap what we've read so far. In the beginning, Jesus was an unknown to everybody but John the Baptist. He calls some followers, and does some healings that make Him incredibly popular. But as He becomes more popular with the public, the rulers (like the Pharisees) begin to hate Him.

The crowds grow larger and larger. He calls the Twelve Apostles to help preach the Gospel, cure diseases, and expel demons. The Pharisees and Herodians become more and more against Him. Then Herod beheads John the Baptist.

The crowds become enormous. It gets to the point where people are going to Him for miracles rather than message. He tries to take a break among the Gentiles, but even there He is recognized and mobbed. Yet His disciples recognize Him as the Christ, and He reveals His glory in an even deeper way on the mountaintop. And He starts talking about what will happen to Him very shortly — death and resurrection.

In the beginning of today's reading, Jesus tries to move in secret because He is instructing His disciples. He knows that He is not going to be on earth much longer, the death of John the Baptist was a strong reminder of that. He is more concerned with teaching the Twelve so that they can continue His ministry after He is gone. And He wants to prepare them for what is to come.

Clearly, they still didn't get it. Like children, they started to have an argument about who was the greatest disciple. And so, He teaches them a few lessons about what it means to be a disciple of Jesus Christ.

First, the "greatest" is the one who is the most humble, most serving. He uses the analogy of serving children, and for a Middle-Eastern man of 2,000 years ago that was quite a shocking statement. Children were raised by women, and usually women and children were considered beneath the dignity of older men. He tells them that when you serve the least, you are serving Him.

Second, anyone can be a disciple. It's not an exclusive club. Jesus is not empowering them for the Twelve for their own sakes, but He is empowering them to empower others. "Anyone who is not against us is for us."

Third, people who are generous to Christ's disciples are generous to Christ. It compliments the first point. The disciples serve others to serve Christ, and others serve the disciples to serve Christ. The point is that everybody serves one another out of love for Jesus. We should serve and allow ourselves to be served, all in the name of God.

> Jesus uses strong imagery to make a point: as a disciple, you must destroy the things in your life that lead you from God.

But He warns of the danger of leading others astray, and tells the disciples to cut off anything in their lives that would keep them or others from the kingdom. No saint has ever physically cut of a body part or taken this passage literally. Jesus uses strong imagery to make a point: as a disciple, you must destroy the things in your life that lead you from God. Otherwise, you will not only sin yourself, but lead others into sin as well. Don't you know that people are watching you? "Bobby's a Christian, but he gets drunk, so why can't I?" You are to be an example for holiness, not an excuse for sin.

FOOD FOR THOUGHT

Salt was used as a preservative in times before refrigeration. Jesus is telling us that we should be the element that keeps things "fresh" rather than allow things to decay. What must you cut out of your life to keep "fresh" in Christ, and bring His life to the world?

Mark 10:1-34

At this point, the Pharisees don't even care about the truth, they're just trying to trap Jesus. Moses allowed people to divorce each other, but that's because they were so "hard hearted." Jesus makes it clear that marriage is forever, and even if they get a legal divorce they are still married in God's eyes. Marriage is not two people agreeing to live with each other; it's a unification of man, woman, and God. It is a reflection of the life of the Trinity. It's not about people discarding each other when they have no "use" for them anymore. It's about sacrifice and completely giving your life to another.

While speaking, children were being brought to Him and the Apostles tried to stop them. After all, Jesus was arguing with Pharisees about marriage, divorce, and adultery. *Surely*, they thought, *this was a serious moment that shouldn't be interrupted by children.* Jesus got upset with them. "Let the little children come to me," He said. Don't forget this picture of Jesus, who would rather embrace a child in love than argue theology with a religious leader.

> Marriage is not two people agreeing to live with each other; it's a unification of man, woman, and God.

As they left that place, a young man fell on his knees and asked what he had to do to inherit eternal life. Clearly, this was a good person, and Jesus "was filled with love for him." But his actions weren't enough. He needed to sacrifice. Notice Jesus didn't say, "Just give everything up and live in poverty by yourself," but "Go and sell what you own... then come, follow me." This man was being called as a *disciple*! He was being called to greatness. But he didn't accept because he was too attached to the world.

I think it's fitting that the world never knew his name. There are many nameless people who didn't give their all for God. But the ones who do have names, the world never forgets: Peter, Paul, Francis of Assisi, Therese of Lisieux...

The disciples were shocked to hear Jesus mention that riches made it hard to follow God, because the Jewish understanding at the time was that the richer you were, the more God loved you. Jesus took a common misconception and (as He did often) turned the model upside down to reveal their blindness and God's goodness. *Following me isn't about what you get, it's about what you give.*

But God makes it clear that He can't be outdone in generosity. Anything we give up for Jesus we will receive 100 times over by God. All that we leave we will receive in abundance (and that includes persecutions, too). But we do not give to *get*, we give for the sake of Jesus and the Gospel He preached.

Everything we read today is about *sacrifice* and *redemption*. A married couple should sacrifice for each other to be united with God. A rich man should sacrifice his possessions to get the joy of being a disciple. Someone who sacrifices their house, family, or land will receive 100 times more for it. And Jesus will sacrifice His life so that He can be resurrected after three days.

It is what Jesus meant when He said, "Many who are first will be last, and the last, first." Jesus turned everything around. As the Gospel was spread, prostitutes became saints and murderers became martyrs, because "nothing is impossible with God." And the "holy people" were the ones who would crucify Christ. At the center of it all was a homeless man who could calm storms with a word and would stop to hug children.

This is the Jesus who is asking us to sacrifice our lives so that we can be with Him. A man and wife leave their family to become one flesh. God became flesh so that we could share in His life. We find our life when we give it away. It's what our relationship with Jesus is about.

FOOD FOR THOUGHT

Mother Teresa had a sign she hung in one of her shelters: "Take what He gives to you, give what He takes from you, and always with a smile." What are you called to sacrifice that will bring you into a closer relationship with God?

Mark 10:35-52

There are two things today's Scripture tells us: be humble and pray big. James and John have the "pray big" part down, but not the "be humble." They ask a huge request of Jesus — to sit at His right and left when He comes in glory. While the other disciples got mad at them for asking such a thing, it's interesting to note that Jesus didn't. He likes big prayer requests.

But they missed the humility. They wanted to rule over others, not to serve them. So Jesus challenged them: do you think you deserve this request? Do you think that you can live up to this challenge? Their answer was *yes*.

I bet that made Jesus smile. They were actually right, for once. They *would* give their lives to serve Jesus. But He told them that it wasn't up to Him to decide. And here we see a picture of the humility of Jesus. He lets the Father decide who would be glorified through His second coming. It's not up to Him.

The others mock James and John, but Jesus uses His own example to once again teach them about what it means to a leader: "The Son of Man Himself came not to be served but to serve" (Mark 10:45). I mean, think about it. If you could choose your life before you were brought into this earth, wouldn't you rather have been a prince than a poor man? A king instead of a carpenter? Would you not have orchestrated your life to end in comfort instead of a cross?

But Jesus didn't come *to be served*, but *to serve*. We continue to see how humble He is when He talks to Bartimaeus, the blind man. Bartimaeus was yelling by the side of the road, but the crowd was telling him to be quiet. Jesus calls him over, and asks this odd question, "What do you want me to do for you?" I'm sure it baffled the crowds. I mean, he was *blind. Couldn't Jesus have figured this out without asking?* But Jesus only went where He was invited. His question gave dignity to this beggar in a way he could have experienced before. The God of the universe stopped to ask a beggar how He could be of help.

And the blind man asked to see. Stop and think for a moment how big that request was. He didn't ask to partially see, or have some help seeing. He didn't say, "If you can," as though he was unsure of Jesus' ability. He screamed at the top of his voice and endured the scorn of the crowds because he *knew* that Christ could cure him.

> Be humble and pray big. You will see the face of Christ.

It was an amazing act of faith. And the next thing that happened was that he went from living in darkness to staring at the face of Jesus.

Be humble and pray big. You will see the face of Christ. Bartimaeus showed his humility by crying out for God. There was no pretense of superiority, nor was his request based on a desire to be better than others. He wanted to see Jesus, but couldn't. He admitted his weakness and was healed. And how did He use this gift of sight? To follow Jesus along the road.

Jesus humbled himself to the blind man, and the blind man humbled himself towards Jesus. They both served each other: one gave sight, the other used that sight to follow Him. It's a perfect picture of how it's supposed to be between us and God.

FOOD FOR THOUGHT

When you pray, do you pray with a humble spirit, looking to serve God rather than lift up yourself? When you make requests, are they bold and full of faith?

The Background

Jesus has made it clear what will happen to Him. He now enters into Jerusalem, the headquarters of the Jewish faith and the dwelling place of His most powerful enemies. As the week progresses, we clearly see how deep the conflict between Jesus and the leaders at the time had become. The account also speaks to us, however, about how we are to behave in a world that is so often against us.

In our battle of faith, we need the help of our entire community to stay strong: those on earth and those in heaven. The book of Revelation talks about Michael, the head of God's army of angels. In this prayer, we pray for him and ask him to pray for us.

Prayer of the Week: *Prayer to St. Michael the Archangel*

St. Michael the Archangel, defend us into battle
Be our protection against the wickedness and snares of the devil
May God rebuke him, we humbly pray
And to you, O prince of the heavenly hosts
By the power of God
Cast into hell Satan and all the evil spirits
Who prowl about the world seeking the ruin of souls.
Amen.

What's Up with Saints?

We believe that those who live in eternity are active in bringing God's kingdom to earth. They do it by *intercession*, lifting their requests before God. They don't have magic powers, they are our prayer partners. They kneel beside us and add their voice to ours. Scripture tells us that, "The prayer of a righteous man has great power in its effects" (James 5:16). How much more "righteous" could you be than standing in the presence of God?

Mark 11:1-25

And so Jesus arrives in Jerusalem, the home of the Jewish faith — the capital of the kingdom of Israel. He enters through the city gates riding a colt (a young male horse). People are throwing their cloaks on the road before him, and others are waving branches. And they are all shouting, "Hosanna! Blessed is He who comes in the name of the Lord!" This marks another dramatic turn in Jesus' ministry. Remember that He disappeared from the Jewish public after the feeding of the five thousand so that He could prepare His disciples. Now He was back with the crowds, and they were cheering His name.

> In the heart of Jerusalem was the Temple. Not a temple, *the* Temple. It was built on the rock where Abraham was willing to sacrifice his son out of obedience to God.

You have to understand the significance of Jerusalem for a Jew to appreciate why this moment was so special. In the heart of Jerusalem was the Temple. Not *a* temple, *the* Temple. It was built on the rock where Abraham was willing to sacrifice his son out of obedience to God. God stopped him, but Abraham's willingness made him their "father in faith." And it was the beginning of God revealing to the Jews how He loved them and was going to save them. Not only that, but within the temple was the "Holy of Holies," where God dwelt. The Temple wasn't just another church, it was *the* Church. Imagine if there wasn't a Catholic Church in every town, but there was only one church building with one tabernacle. That's what it was like for the Jews.

All Jews made pilgrimages to the Temple to bring animal sacrifices to God. But when they got there, they were in for a surprise. Whatever animal they brought for sacrifice was deemed unworthy by the Temple authorities, so they had to buy a new one. And they had to buy it with Jewish currency, which nobody had since the Romans had taken over. So they would have to go to the money changers, who would exchange it for Jewish money at an unfair rate. Then they would have to buy a new animal at an outrageously high price.

It was a scam, but nobody had the courage to do anything about it. Until Jesus walked in. People who think Jesus was just a "nice guy" or a "wimp" should read about Him driving out the sellers and knocking over tables, screaming at them at the top of his voice. Animals were running, birds were flying, money was rattling across the ground, and people were running for their lives from this mad man who was saying something about this being "My Father's house." He was just a poor carpenter's son from Galilee; a "hick" compared to the city dwellers. *Where does He get off thinking He owns the place?*

I'm sure those were the thoughts of the Pharisees as they watched Him act, but they were too afraid to do anything because He was so popular with the crowds. Jesus left the temple and went back to Bethany, which was right outside the city. And that's when Peter noticed the fig tree.

This was no coincidence — Jesus used the fig tree to teach His disciples what was going on. The fig tree had leaves but no fruit. That wasn't good enough for God. The leaves gave an outward appearance of life, but the lack of fruit showed that it wasn't real. That's what the religious leaders were like. And their time of "fruitlessness" was over.

Nothing is impossible with faith, Jesus concludes. Fig trees will wither and mountains will move. You just need to believe God and forgive others. That's how prayers get answered. And that's how Jesus will free His people.

FOOD FOR THOUGHT

In your life do you have leaves but no fruit? Are there times you "fake" it? Who do you need to forgive in order to receive forgiveness?

Mark 11:27-12:12

Now that Jesus is in Jerusalem, the heart of the Jewish faith, it will be helpful to explain who the people are that we read about today so you can have a better understanding of what is going on.

The "chief priests" were the servants of the Temple at Jerusalem. Since God was in the Temple and the priests served God, you would only find them there. They were in charge of offering sacrifices, and were the only ones who could go into the "Holy of Holies."

The scribes were the educated, the elite. They were the ones who were the smartest, brightest, and most listened to by the Jewish people. Since much of the public couldn't read or write (like most of the world at the time), they had great power because they were some of the few who could read God's law, and they would interpret it for the people of the time.

This is their first encounter with this mysterious man who roamed among the peasants and was said to perform miracles. They were probably quite upset when He cleared the Temple the day earlier, and their question to Him was, "Who told you that you can act this way?" It wasn't a real question, it was an accusation.

Jesus turned the tables on them. He told them that He had an answer to their question, but they had to answer one of His first. He asked them about His cousin, John the Baptist, who they were so much against. So they argued about how they should answer, and ended up not answering His question at all. So Jesus didn't answer theirs.

This was the sin of the priests — they had no *integrity*. Think of integrity as "who you are when no one is looking." Your true character comes out in private. Publicly speaking, though, integrity is seen when you say what you mean and mean what you say. It's interesting that Jesus didn't say, "I'll talk to you if you tell me that God sent John the Baptist." He said, "Tell me what you thought about John." The priests didn't believe in John the Baptist, and they wouldn't admit it. So they missed out on Jesus' teaching about Himself.

I really think that if they were honest with Jesus, Jesus would have been honest with them. He never seemed to have a problem with people who didn't believe, but He had a real problem with people who weren't honest. Our God is one who doesn't like to play games. He would waste no time with people who couldn't stand up for what they believed.

> God cannot reveal Himself to a person who cares only about what others think. Jesus never tried to win a popularity contest. He was who He was. And He made us who we are.

He went on to talk about them, and in His parable summed up much of what happened in the Old Testament. The prophets of God were persecuted by such people, and were usually killed for their faith. Jesus is telling them that their time is up.

How did they respond? The same way they always did, with cowardice. They were more concerned with what other people thought than to do what they thought was right (even though they were wrong). In the book of Revelation, we hear Jesus say to a group of people, "I know your works: you are neither cold nor hot." I wish you were one or the other (Revelation 3:15). God cannot reveal Himself to a person who cares only about what others think. Jesus never tried to win a popularity contest. He was who He was. And He made us who we are. He is big enough to handle our questions and our doubts. It's only when we ask them that we can get answers.

FOOD FOR THOUGHT

Are you honest with God? Do you have integrity before Him and those around you?

Mark 12:13-34

The priests and scribes failed to trick Jesus, so they sent in the Herodians, the Pharisees, and the Sadduccees. The Herodians were a purely political group (that supported King Herod), while the Pharisees and the Sadduccees represented two streams of Jewish thought. The Pharisees believed in an extremely strict interpretation of God's law. The Sadduccees were so liberal they didn't even believe in such basic teachings as the resurrection of the dead.

Like the priests and scribes, they all tried to trap Him. The Pharisees and Herodians hoped that He would publicly tell people not to pay the tax, and then would report Him to the Roman soldiers who would arrest Him. But Jesus was smarter than that. He asked them who made the coins, they replied, "Caesar." So He said, "Pay Caesar what belongs to Caesar... and God what belongs to God." People who are citizens of heaven can't forget that they are temporarily residing on earth. We can't use serving God as an excuse to neglect our human obligations.

> People who are citizens of heaven can't forget that they are temporarily residing on earth. We can't use serving God as an excuse to neglect our human obligations.

Next came the Sadducces with the wedding question. Jesus *slams* them: "Is not this why you are wrong, that you know neither the Scriptures nor the power of God?" Remember, the Sadducces didn't even believe there would be a resurrection in the first place, and so the only reason they could possibly ask is so that they could make Jesus look stupid. But Jesus turned the tables once again, and they went away like the priests, scribes, Pharisees, and Herodians did: *humiliated.*

But finally, there came a real question. Not all scribes were so bent on their own agenda that they wouldn't listen to the Truth. And Jesus answered him honestly, and even commended him for his response to it (a fascinating response we'll talk more about in the next section).

Jesus held His ground even in the face of the most popular, most respected, and most powerful people. He would not tolerate those who tried to trap Him, but would answer any question from a seeking heart. There is no dumb question from the person who truly seeks Him. That is who He came to speak to. That is who He came to save.

"He is not God of the dead, but of the living" (Luke 20:38). Jesus wasn't preaching about rules and regulations. He was talking about how to have a living relationship with God. That's why the scribe's question at the end was so good — it dealt with how to be a follower of God, rather than use God's law for his own advantage.

There are two kinds of questions we are asked about our faith. Some people ask to prove us wrong. Others ask to find what is right. In defending your faith, you should know that *why* a person asks a question is usually more important than *what* a person asks. Although many might just try to trick you, there are many who truly want to know the truth. It would have been easy to think the final question was another attack. Like Jesus, we might have to endure traps to get to a real question, but no matter what is asked we should answer it like Jesus did: **correctly** (which means we must learn the answers), **honestly** (Jesus knew everything, sure, but it's okay for you to say, "I don't know, but I'll find out"), and **boldly** (when you know it, then say it!).

FOOD FOR THOUGHT

How do you respond when people ask you about your faith? Do you proclaim it correctly, boldly, and honestly, even if people might not like what you say?

Mark 12:28-44

I know it's easier to use your imagination when Jesus is walking on water or curing a leper, but don't forget to use it as He teaches the people. Scripture tells us that all of this transpired before "a great crowd," and that they listened to Him with "delight." Imagine how cool it must have been to see this man they had heard about from others and now got to see Him in the flesh. Imagine the looks on the faces of those who tried to trick Him, but ended up looking pretty foolish when they tried.

Jesus explains a confusing passage of Scripture to the crowd. Since the Christ was the son of David, why would David call him Lord? The scribes could never answer it, but Jesus could: the Christ is not only human, but the one who created humanity.

But the real message of what Jesus talked about was *total commitment*. How do we love God? With *all* our heart, with *all* our strength, with *all* our mind, and with *all* our strength. St. Therese of Lisieux once said, "No one can be half a saint." We have got to give Him everything we have if we are to live the life He is offering to us. You can't have one foot on the boat and one foot on the dock. You'll just end up in the water.

The biggest reason I see people walk away from the faith is that they don't make the full commitment. Like the chief priests of the time, they give themselves permission to not live up to the Gospel calling. They'll accept *most* of what Jesus teaches, but not *all* of it — particularly those parts that call them to sacrifice and change.

There is a difference between those who are Catholic by *choice* and Catholic by *coincidence*. Those who are Catholic "by coincidence" are people who think there is a God who loves them, Mass is good, and Jesus was wise are happy to find that the Church teaches the same things they already believe. But what about those challenging issues: Going to mass every Sunday? Saving sex for marriage? Fasting from meat? Loving your enemies? Sacrificing your life? Those who come to the Church by *coincidence* often think those aspects aren't needed, and that they only have to follow "parts" of the Gospel (usually, the easy ones). They are happy to walk with Jesus in the way they are already heading, but when He turns to head towards the cross, they just wave goodbye.

We are all called to give 100%. It is the only way that God can be God. It's like this: God is an engine of a car. You can't put the engine on the wheel — it won't work and it will make you miserable. But many times people try to put God as an accessory to their life, instead of the center of it. In another Gospel, Jesus says this about the Father, "Seek first His kingdom and His righteousness, and all these things shall be yours as well" (Matthew 6:33). It's what Jesus has been talking about all along: we find our life when we give it to God.

The wonderful thing about God is that He works on percentages, rather than on price. There's a big difference between something that costs $1,000,000 and something that costs everything you have in our pocket. The story of the widow emphasizes that God is *affordable* — everybody can receive Him. How much does following God cost? The price would be too high, we couldn't afford it. So He tells us to empty our pockets and give us what we have. There isn't anybody who can't afford 100%. He only wants our all.

FOOD FOR THOUGHT

Have you been loving Him with your *all*? If not, what is holding you back from loving Him 100%? Is your Catholic faith a choice you have made?

Mark 13:1-13

Jesus lays down some heavy news to the Apostles. Jerusalem will be destroyed. The Temple will be completely gone.

Imagine the shock this must have been. They went from marveling at the beauty of the Temple to hearing that soon it will be no more. Remember the Jewish connection to the Temple and its supreme importance: it's the place on earth where God dwelt. It was the ultimate Church, the home for God built by Solomon 1,000 years earlier, and rebuilt 500 years ago. Even the horror that Americans felt, for instance, when the World Trade Center was destroyed on September 11, 2001, would pale in comparison to the devastation experienced by the Jews at the loss of their Temple (as well as their entire city). Yet Jesus tells them that it will happen, and they are eager to know when.

Jesus lays it out plainly before His disciples: there are hard times ahead. Yet He tells them four things to do to face this crisis.

"Take care that no one deceives you." —
- Many times, people are quick to see horrible things as the end of the world. But sadly, there is more to come. In fact, Jesus says that it is just "the beginning of the birth-pangs." In a sense, Jesus brings new life to the world, and the world must go through the pains of labor to bring it to fruition.

"Be on your guard." —
- People will be out to get them because of their faith. They will be brought before all sorts of people, but that's how the faith will spread.

"Do not worry." —
- The Holy Spirit will tell them what to say when those times come. They must be at peace with the confidence of God who will be present with them.

"Stand firm."—
- They shouldn't be surprised that they will be hated but know that "anyone who stands firm to the end will be saved."

About 40 years later, the Roman emperor Titus conquered and ravaged Jerusalem. The Temple was totally destroyed. The city was left in ruins. It's citizens fled to the hills and surrounding areas. The prophesy came true.

But what Jesus tells us is more than something of the past; it is something of the present. History will bring about similar trials that plague different generations, but He tells us how to handle them as people of faith and proclaimers of the Gospel. We should be not deceived, be on our guard, be not afraid, and stand firm.

> Remember the Jewish connection to the Temple and its supreme importance: it's the place on earth where God dwelt.

Moments of crisis are opportunities for growth in faith. It's when we see such destruction that we realize how fragile we are and how much we need God. We see shootings on campuses, terrorist attacks, senseless acts of violence and persecution constantly. What is the next crisis around the corner? We don't know what they might be, but we do know how to handle them: in faith.

FOOD FOR THOUGHT

Buildings don't need to be destroyed to create devastation in a person's life. The death of a loved one, divorce, serious sickness, or many other things can shatter the stability that we so often cling to. How can Jesus' advice to the disciples help you?

Mark 13:14-37

Jesus begins by talking about the Temple. He ends by talking about the end of the world.

I'm in my 40's and I can share with you that in my life the world was supposed to end about five times or so. At least that's what fortune-tellers and visionaries have claimed, false visions, or someone who found some "secret message in the Bible." Many thought that the world would end at the year 2000; others predicted 2012. Apparently, they also thought that way right when the first millennium rolled around (1000 A.D.). It was even reported, back then, that there were people who were so anxious about it, that they had heart attacks and died as the church bells rang in the new year.

Do you know what was one of the top food items sold right before the year 2000? Powered milk. People were convinced there would be some kind of disaster, and so they prepared for survival. What fools! (By the way, if anyone needs some powered milk I've got a basement full of it.)

Honestly though, I never thought the world would end on January 1, 2000 or December 21, 2012 because that would be too *predictable*. Jesus makes it clear that we won't know the time or the hour. But don't be confused: the world *will* end. In fact, it might even end before you finish reading this page. Are you ready?

Jesus isn't trying to scare His followers; He's just preparing them for reality. The things of this earth pass away, but He is eternal. He came to the world in humility, but He will return in glory. We should be mindful of the temporary place this world is, so that we can keep our mind on heavenly things.

We are told to "stay awake." We don't know the hour of the end of the world, or the hour of our own death. We must focus on our relationship with God *now*, because most people die sooner than they think they will. As Christians, this shouldn't lead us into despair but hope. We have an eternal destiny that lies far beyond the pettiness of this world. And much of what we worry about in this life doesn't matter in the next.

Since we know how things will end, it should help give focus to our lives. If everything in this world will pass away, then why do we spend so much time focusing on the temporary than the eternal? The early Church was fueled with the thought that Jesus would return any minute. But as the years passed, the followers wondered why Jesus hadn't shown up yet. St. Peter (our first Pope) wrote to them, "Since all these things are thus to be dissolved, what sort of persons ought you to be in lives of holiness and godliness... count the forbearance of our Lord as salvation" (2 Peter 3:11,15). It's almost 2000 years later, and He still hasn't come. Don't think He isn't going to show up, but realize that He waits so that we can grow in holiness and proclaim the good news.

If you have made it to the end of this page and the world hasn't ended, then it's because He is giving you another opportunity to draw closer to Him and spread His Gospel. Don't fall asleep by thinking everything is fine and nothing will ever change. Remember: You are living on borrowed time, so use it well.

FOOD FOR THOUGHT

How are you distracted (or even consumed) by the temporary things of this earth? How can you spend more time on eternal things?

Mark 14:1-21

Our Gospel reading today focuses on two people, and how they relate to Jesus. The first is the woman who anoints Him with oil. The other is the one who will betray Him.

When a person died back then, the people would cover the dead body with extremely aromatic oils. The more rich or famous the person was, the better the oil. This woman brings in the best, and covers Him with it. Jesus was about to die the death of a criminal, not the kind of death that someone like Him deserved. As a criminal, they would wrap His body in a cloth and throw it in an unmarked grave. This woman was extravagant in her actions towards Jesus, so much so it caused those around Him to question if there wasn't a better use of her money. But it wasn't just *anyone* who raised the question. The Gospel of John gives us a bit more detail to this story:

But Judas Iscariot, one of His disciples (he who was to betray Him), said, "Why was this ointment not sold for three hundred denarii and given to the poor?" This he said, not that he cared for the poor but because he was a thief, and as he had the money box he used to take what was put into.

One person comes to Jesus to give abundantly. The other sees Him as an opportunity for their own gain. The woman's action has been remembered in honor for over 2,000 years, while Judas' betrayal is considered one of the worst acts ever done.

> When a person died back then, the people would cover the dead body with extremely aromatic oils. The more rich or famous the person was, the better the oil.

Jesus comments that it would be better "if he had never been born." But don't think that means that Jesus hated him. In fact, He called Judas to be one of the Twelve! Judas spent time with Jesus, ate with Him, and empowered Him. When the disciples were sent out to preach the Gospel, cure sicknesses, and cast out demons, Judas was right there doing it with them. There were probably people who came to know Jesus because of Judas' preaching!

Judas knew Jesus more intimately than anyone in history, and that's what makes his betrayal so horrible. Why did he do it? He was a thief. He was in it for himself. He wanted to *use* God, not *serve* God. Simply put, he was the kind of person of whom Jesus said, "For whoever would save his life will lose it" (Mark 8:35).

What a remarkable contrast to the woman who appears to anoint Jesus. She thinks of nothing for herself, she just *gives*. And for the first time in His adult life, someone treats Him with the kind of royalty He truly deserves.

It is interesting how people will waste so much on worldly things but be stingy with God. They'll drop $50 at the mall without thinking, but really contemplate if they should put $5 in the Church collection. Some teens I minister to get looked down upon because they participate in our Church youth group two or even three times a week, but others who spend every waking hour on a high school sport are praised.

This double standard is prevalent in almost every aspect of our culture, and even existed in the Jewish culture back then. But the woman didn't care. She cared for Jesus so much that it was *embarrassing*, and made even the disciples feel awkward. Yet she will never be forgotten for her gift to God. We've already talked about giving 100% to God. This woman gave one hundred and ten.

FOOD FOR THOUGHT

Where do you find yourself being stingy with God? How can you be extravagant for Him?

PART FIVE

The Background

I want to forewarn you that this part of the Gospel will be the most wonderful and the most difficult thing you will ever read. You have probably known that Jesus dies, but that fact becomes quite different once you know Jesus personally. It's the difference between hearing that a tragedy happened to a stranger or that a tragedy happened to a close friend. We will share in the horror, but also rejoice in the Resurrection. It's what our faith is about.

Your prayer for the week is simple, but profound. It should be repeated often, as often as you want to tell Jesus you love Him. It's the kind of prayer that you can say as you walk around your house, stand at work, or kneel in prayer. It's called the "Jesus Prayer." And it goes like this:

Prayer for the Week: *The Jesus Prayer*

Jesus, Son of God, have mercy on me, a sinner.

Didn't I Just Say That?

Many times in prayer, we repeat ourselves. That's because we are involved with sharing our heart, not just our mind. Our mind would state the fact once, and leave it at that. Our heart seeks to recreate the emotion behind what we say, and say it over and over again. Prayers to God are not facts, but kisses. We want to give Him lots of them, over and over to show our affection. That's why we'll say three Our Fathers, 50 Hail Marys, or keep repeating the Jesus prayer. It's not just an example of our knowledge; it's an expression of our love.

The same is true when you hear about Jesus. You might have heard the story before, but that shouldn't matter because it's not about information, but an *encounter*. We are not meant to hear the story of His death and resurrection just once, and then bury it in our mind as some sort of historical fact. Every time we hear anything about the faith is a chance to encounter Jesus, even if we think we've heard it all before. You are not reading to *learn*, but praying to *love*. Keep that in prayer through this last week.

Mark 14:22-25

There isn't much to read today, but there is a lot to think about. What Jesus just did is the *source and summit* of our Catholic faith.

Remember how powerful the words of Jesus are. He would tell the demons to flee, and it would happen. He would tell a dead girl to get up, and it would happen. The voice that spoke, "Let there be light" in the beginning of the Bible was *Jesus*. He speaks, and things happen by the power of His Word. Light is created. Demons are cast out. The dead are raised. And bread and wine become His body and blood.

> The Church doesn't see the Eucharist as a symbol. It is the real presence of Jesus Christ: body, blood, soul, and divinity.

The Church calls the celebration of this the "Eucharist," and that word comes from the phrase "to give thanks," which is what Jesus did as He broke the bread and poured the wine. The Church doesn't see the Eucharist as a symbol. It is the real presence of Jesus Christ: body, blood, soul, and divinity. Does it still look like bread? Yes, just as Jesus still looked human even though we recognize Him as God. He transformed bread and wine into His body and blood. And He invited His followers to share it with Him.

One of the most distinctive things about the Catholic faith is how we celebrate the Eucharist. It is the high point of every Mass, and the reason we gather together as a community on Sundays. It's not about how good the homily or the music is (or isn't). No matter how bad or boring a particular Mass you are at is, it doesn't change the miracle of the transformation of bread and wine to the body and blood of Jesus Christ.

But we not only can worship Jesus in the Eucharist, we also receive Him. What an incredible gift! It is our closest moment with God that we can get before we live eternally in His presence in heaven.

It makes sense that Jesus would have the power to celebrate the Eucharist, but how does the Church? We see that elsewhere in Scripture. The same voice that said "Let there be light" and "This is my body," said to the Apostles, "Do this in remembrance of me" (1 Corinthians 11:24). That was the beginning of the sacrament we call Holy Orders, the sacrament of the priesthood. Jesus gave the Apostles the gift to celebrate this miracle with others, and they in turn have passed down that anointing over 2,000 years until it ended up empowering your local parish priest.

If someone gave you a gift right before they died, it would probably be a very special thing. The Eucharist is His gift to you, the way He continues to always be with us and allows us to see, touch, and even taste His love for us. Sound weird? The Gospel of John tells that many left Jesus because they didn't understand His foretelling of the Eucharist (John 6:48-66). Haven't you read enough of the life of Jesus to realize that He usually reveals Himself in ways you wouldn't expect?

FOOD FOR ~~THOUGHT~~ YOUR SOUL!

The next time you are at Mass, think about what it is that you are invited to receive. The next time you are at Church, realize the real presence of Jesus in the tabernacle where the Eucharist is kept. If you can, go there and spend some time adoring Him.

Mark 14:26-52

"And when they had sung a hymn," is how this reading opens up. I don't know if we usually imagine a Jesus who liked to sing, but He did. There is an entire book of psalms in the Old Testament; they were all songs that were dedicated to God. And there Jesus stood, singing them with His friends. Seeing as how Jesus put everything into what He did, I bet He sang them at the top of His voice. It's just another insight into this person we are trying to know better.

But following that, He gave His closest followers some difficult and heavy news. All the talk of His death was about to happen, and everyone would run away from Him. Judas had already betrayed Him, and the rest will desert Him as well. They all vowed adamantly that it wouldn't occur (particularly Peter), but Jesus knew better. He told them this not to blame them but to give them hope in what was about to be a very dark moment in their lives. "After I am raised up, I will go before you to Galilee." *I know you are going to desert me, but we will be together again.* Even in this moment of great personal suffering, He still cared for and worried about those whom He chose.

> Jesus put God's desires and will before His own, just like He taught us to do when He gave us the "Our Father." (Remember that whole "thy will be done" line?)

The Agony in the Garden makes the horror that is about to happen more real. Yes, Jesus knew that He was going to die. But that doesn't mean He *wanted* to. He was fully God, but also fully human. He was facing torture and execution. He pulled His closest friends to Him, and asked them to stay awake while He prayed for strength. But they couldn't. He prayed to the Father, and shared what He wanted ("Take this cup away from me"), but also loved God enough to accept what He was called to do. Jesus put God's desires and will before His own, just like He taught us to do when He gave us the "Our Father." (Remember that whole "thy will be done" line?)

Could we ask for a better friend than Jesus? Could we hope for a God that we could relate to as much as He? Jesus knew what it was like to do something He didn't want to do for the sake of a greater good. He knew what it was like to have His prayers go unanswered. And He knew what it was like to be hurt by people that He loved.

Judas arrives, and if it wasn't bad enough that he betrayed Jesus, what it worse is how he gives the signal to the soldiers: with a kiss. Swords are drawn and a fight begins, but Jesus stops it and the disciples run away. The "young man" who ran away naked is often attributed to Mark, the Gospel writer himself.

And so Jesus begins in song but ends in solitude, surrounded by those who hated Him. But notice that though He did not want to go, He did not fight it. He embraced what He had to do. He knew of the glory that awaited Him at the end, but that didn't make the suffering any easier. And so the God who came to love was led away in chains by the very people He came to save. The greatest act of love begins.

FOOD FOR THOUGHT

In friendships, we are often drawn to people who have shared similar experiences with us. How have you been betrayed? How have you prayed in a way that has not been answered yet, or not as you had hoped for? How have you been afraid of the future? Take some time to share those things with Jesus.

Mark 14:53-72

Once again, we see that Jesus will not bother with lies, but will always speak the truth. The Sanhedrin was the Jewish court, and it was before this court that Jesus was put on trial. But unlike many trials, where you start with a conviction and then render a verdict, this court began with the verdict and then tried to come up with a crime that would fit.

It must have been quite a scene. The witnesses conflicting each other, people shouting, people arguing, and in the middle of the storm stood Jesus. He quietly watched the circus that surrounded Him. He knew they were going to kill Him, it was just a matter of time. Finally, the high priest quieted everybody and asked, "Are you the Christ, the son of the Blessed One?" He said, "I am."

With this, they began to beat Him and spit at Him. But they couldn't kill Him because of Roman law. Part of the law that Rome passed down after they occupied Jerusalem was that the Jews could have their own courts, but could never execute a prisoner. If someone was to die, they must be found guilty by Roman law first. So they sent Jesus over to Pilate, the head Roman of the area.

> Part of the law that Rome passed down after they occupied Jerusalem was that the Jews could have their own courts, but could never execute a prisoner. If someone was to die, they must be found guilty by Roman law first.

As this was occurring, Peter watched at a distance. You've got to give him some credit — he followed while the others ran. But when he was discovered, he started to renounce knowing Jesus, even to the point of cursing and swearing. And he wept when he heard the cock crow. Peter's sin was that of pride. He thought he could do something Jesus said he couldn't. "Even though they all fall away, I will not," he said. "If I must die with you, I will never deny you."

When the soldiers appeared at the garden, Peter drew a sword and was ready to fight had not Jesus stopped him. I think that many of us would enter such a battle. We would be willing to die for Jesus Christ, should the heroic need arise. But will we live for Him? That's where it gets harder.

We can be drawn to the big, dramatic actions of faith, but what about the little day-to-day stuff? We will go to a weekend retreat, but will we gossip about someone we don't like? We'll attend a service project, but will we spend time in daily prayer? That's where it really counts, and that's what Peter realized as he ran away in tears. *Does it matter what I say to a servant girl?* He probably asked himself. *It's just a little thing.* But as the crowds grew larger and the fear increased, he found he would say just about anything to save his own skin.

This proud man, who hours before was willing to stand up to armed guards, was defeated by a little slave girl. It was because he didn't act like Jesus. When Jesus was asked a question, He spoke the truth, no matter what the consequence was. As Peter saw the results of that truth, he decided that he didn't want that to happen to him.

The other Gospel accounts tell us that Peter repented, but Judas killed himself. They both betrayed Jesus, but it was how they acted *after* that made the difference. One became the world's most famous sinner. The other became our first Pope, and one of the Church's most famous saints.

FOOD FOR THOUGHT

In what "little ways" do you deny Christ? Do you follow Him in the small, everyday things as well as the big?

It is shocking to think how quickly we will trade an imitation for the real thing. We chose a convict over the Christ. The very crowds who were shouting "Hosanna!" on the streets were now shouting, "Crucify him!"

Pilate knew it was a charade, but wanted to be loved by the people. It's amazing how often we turn away from Christ because we want to be loved by others — Pilate is no different. The chief priests kissed up to Pilate to so that he would kill Jesus. Pilate let them do it so that he could kiss up to the crowd. The crowd yelled, "crucify" to kiss up to the priests. Everybody was using everybody else. It was the ultimate example of anti-love. And in the midst of it stood Jesus, sentenced to death.

They whipped His body. They pierced His head with thorns. This scourging was a part of the crucifixion process. It was meant to torture a prisoner so that they'd have no strength to fight by the time they made it to the cross. It most commonly involved a leather whip with sharp pieces of bone and pottery connected to it. The torturer would wrap the whip around the victims' body, then pull. It was said that a person was almost unrecognizable after such a beating, with strips of flesh and muscle torn away with each strike.

But to add an even crueler dimension, the soldiers made a crown of thorns and placed it on His sacred head. They had nothing but loathing for the Jews, and thought it funny that anyone would want to be their "king." They added torment to their torture, by dressing Him up and pretending to worship Him. Then they rose and started to beat Him up again.

Apparently, they were a bit too harsh because they had to enlist a passer-by to help Jesus carry His cross. They would only do this if they were afraid the victim wouldn't make it and die on the road. Simon of Cyrene carried the wood, while the Romans dragged the bloodied and bruised body of Jesus through the cobblestone streets of the city, to the hill called Golgotha where He was to be killed.

FOOD FOR THOUGHT

As hard as it may be, read the Scriptures again and visualize what we did to our Lord. We'd like to think that if we were there we *wouldn't* yell, "Crucify him!" or "We want Barabbas!" But how often do we choose the fake thing over the real? How often do we do things motivated, not by what is right, but by what others want us to do? Today we see what happens when we choose being loved by others over being loved by Him. Ask for His mercy.

Crucifixion was known to all the readers back then, so Mark didn't need to go into any more detail except, "they crucified Him." But since He went through this for us, it would only be right to know what He did, and what they did to Him.

Historians tell us that since the dawn of recorded history, twisted humanity has found no better way to torture and kill a man than crucifixion. Before He took up the cross, Jesus' flesh was mutilated through scourging. They then tied our Lord's hands to the crossbeam and made Him carry it through cobblestone paths to the hill of crucifixion. That was another torture in itself, as the splintered wood almost clotted to His exposed muscles and the soldiers continually knocked Christ down. With His hands tied to the huge piece of wood that bore into His shoulders, Jesus would have had no protection from falling face first into the cold stone beneath Him.

Finally, after a mile or so walk, Jesus arrived at the hill known as Golgatha. They held the Lord down and put a nail through each wrist, and then one nail through the ankles of both feet. Then they tied a rope around His shoulders and pulled, dislocating both of them. The soldiers then dropped the cross into a hole in the ground so it would stand upright, leaving Jesus gasping for air.

> When we make crucifixes of Jesus today, we can't show the true horror of what happened — if we did we would become physically sick every time we walked into a Church.

And that is how our Lord died on the cross — by suffocation. Since His shoulders were dislocated, His lung cage collapsed, and the only way He could get air to breathe was by pulling Himself up on the nails in His hands.

The Romans did not invent crucifixion but they perfected it. Their torture was an art form to them. It was said a person could survive a few days hanging there on a cross, writhing up and down on the wood in immense pain, their skin blue with asphyxiation, gasping for air. People would often give them food or drink, not out of mercy, but to prolong the process of death.

A person hung naked on the cross, only their own blood to cover them. When we make crucifixes of Jesus today, we can't show the true horror of what happened — if we did we would become physically sick every time we walked into a Church. And as He hung there naked, bleeding, and broken... they mocked Him. The chief priests came to gloat over their victory. The passers-by jeered at Him, wondering why a person who could raise the dead couldn't seem to save Himself. Even the others who were crucified joined in.

What held Him to the cross? Surely the Man who told the storm to be quiet could speak and end this horror. But the living Word of God was remarkably silent through this whole process. It was because it was not nails that held Him to the cross, but love. The priests thought they forced this on Him, but the truth is that He *chose* this. He could have stopped it at any time. But He wanted to show the depth of love that He had for us, and emphasize the freedom that He offers everyone, even the freedom to allow His death to happen. He wanted to live out the very thing He had been challenging His disciples with: that to love means to give yourself away.

And so there He hung. Splinters in His back. Thorns in His head. And love that held Him to the wood.

FOOD FOR THOUGHT

Imagine yourself at the foot of the cross. Fall on your knees and thank him for His amazing love.

Mark 15:33-47

What was that?
Is he saying something?
Maybe he is calling for Elijah!

His voice was cracked and dry. Every breath an effort. Those surrounding the cross heard moans from the body that hung there. "Eloi, eloi, lama sabachtani?" They mistook the word "Eloi" for "Elijah." Someone ran to get Him some vinegar so that He could speak better. They wanted to hear what this "great" preacher had to say. But He wasn't saying anything at all.

He was singing.

What came from His mouth was the first line of a psalm that He and all Jews had known since their youth. He could only sing one line, since His throat was dry with blood and every breath required lifting Himself higher on the nails. But that brief line tells us what was going on in His head before He took His last breath.

"My God, my God, why have you forsaken me?" is the beginning of Psalm 22. Some think that this means He lost hope, or felt abandoned by God. But that's not what the psalm is about. Psalm 22 begins with a person who feels despair, but ends with an unfailing confidence in God. Written hundreds of years prior, it describes the very things He went through that day, and what it all meant:

My God, my God, why have you forsaken me?
My strength is trickling away
My bones are all disjointed
My heart as turned to wax, melting inside me
My mouth is as dry as earthenware,
My tongue sticks to my jaw
You lay me down in the dust of death
A gang of villains is closing in on me
As if to hack off my hands and feet
I can count every one of my bones
While they look on and gloat

Yahweh, do not hold aloof!
My strength, come quickly to my help
I shall proclaim your name to my brothers,
Praise you in full assembly
For he has not despised nor disregarded the poverty of the poor
Has not turned away his face, but has listened to the cry for help
The whole wide world will remember and return to Yahweh
All families of nations bow down before him
And those who are dead, their descendants will serve him,
Will proclaim his name to generations still to come
And these will tell of his saving justice to a people yet unborn:
He has fulfilled it

As He breathed His last, the veil of the sanctuary was torn in two from top to bottom. This was the cloth that separated the Holy of Holies from the rest of the people. The symbolism here is important. The thing that physically separated God and His people was now split in two by His death upon the cross, just as the sin that spiritually separated God and His children was now destroyed. Jesus died for our sins. He embraced death so that we can have life. And there is no one who can't receive this gift.

How incredible it is that the very first person to acknowledge Jesus as the Son of God... was *the same man* who only hours ordered nails driven through His sacred hands! And God still loved him. Think about that for a moment and all that it teaches us. There is nothing you can do that would make God not love you. Since the beginning of Scripture, God had promised to find a way to bring His people back to Him. We are the *people yet unborn* to whom the Psalm refers to, and by dying upon the cross *He has fulfilled* that promise. This was the message He tried to sing to us as He gave His last breath and died.

They took His body off the cross, and laid it in a tomb donated by Joseph of Arimathaea, one of

> As He breathed His last, the veil of the sanctuary was torn in two from top to bottom. This was the cloth that separated the Holy of Holies from the rest of the people.

the few good members of the Sanhedrin. They rolled a rock in front of it and went home, since it was about to be the Sabbath and they were not allowed to do anything more.

FOOD FOR THOUGHT

Take a moment to imagine yourself before the cross, and commit your life to the person hanging there. It does not matter what you have done or where you have been. He has destroyed the barrier of sin that was between us, but has not taken away our freedom. He has made His love available. The choice is up to us.

Mark 16:1-20

That Sabbath brought no joy for the followers of Jesus. The person they followed for years, the one they had put all their hope upon, the only one who ever called them to be something more what than they were... was dead. I'm sure Peter thought about going back to his boat. I'm sure Matthew wondered if he could be a tax collector again.

Three women came to the tomb to give the body of Jesus the oils and spices that were proper for burial. They had rushed to get His corpse into the tomb before the Sabbath began, so that it wouldn't rot under the hot Jerusalem sun. They headed there, unsure of how they were to complete their task since the rock they sealed the tomb with was very large. But when they arrived, the rock had been rolled away.

Who would dare to open the tomb? Has someone done something with the body? They entered and to their surprise they saw a young man in a white robe who told them that the world would never be the same. "He has risen, He is not here."

It is no wonder that they were shocked to hear the news. Our society has a saying: it was *too good to be true.* Jesus risen from the dead? *Too good to be true.* Our sins forgiven, no matter what we've done? *Too good to be true.* We are called not as slaves but as children? *Too good to be true.*

That phrase is not one we have received from heaven, but learned from earth. It is why the Eleven were so slow to believe that it actually happened. But from God, there is no such thing as "too good to be true." There is just *good*, and there is just *true*. God is good *and* true, and the life He offers us is the same.

Jesus commands His followers to do two things: *go* and *proclaim*. They are both very difficult things to do. To *go* means to not stay where you are, and that's hard for us because we generally don't like change. It means we find ourselves in new situations. It means we feel uncomfortable. It means we don't always know where we'll end up. It means we build relationships with people we might not normally get to know (or even like). It means we follow Jesus wherever He leads us.

The second command is to *proclaim*. We do this with our words, and we do this with our lives. Wherever we *go*, by word or deed, we are to be a witness to the empty tomb and the risen Christ. There is a world that is in desperate need of this message. And this message is for *everyone*, no matter where they're from, who they are, or how long they've been living.

Go and *proclaim*. Miraculous signs will follow you as you do. You are entrusted with the greatest news that can ever be told, one that is *good* and *true*. Once again, Jesus did the unexpected. The cross, which used to be the symbol of death and torture, is now a symbol of faith and life. If He can turn an instrument of death into the pathway to eternity, then imagine what He can do with you.

There are three other Gospels you should read: the Gospel according to Matthew, the Gospel according to Luke, and the Gospel according to John. But the most important Gospel is the way you live your life for Jesus Christ: the Gospel according to you. You are to become a living Gospel for the entire world to read. You bring this Gospel to life by everything you say and do. Every day becomes another page to proclaim His love for the world. Every sin becomes another opportunity to share His grace. You need not be perfect to share the Gospel. If that were so, then no one could have ever spoken the message to anyone else. You just have to be willing to *go* and *proclaim* that there is a God who loves sinful people, and can save them no matter what they have done. Use your life as continual example of that mercy.

For what you read was not about a God who *lived* but a God who *lives*. Jesus is risen and He loves you. He wants a relationship with you. So live in His love, and grow in His grace. You know Him better now, which means that you can love Him more. Do not persist in the sin that caused His death, but "turn around" so that you can embrace His life. He will give you the grace to do it, and will pick you up every time you fall. Continue to seek the face of Christ in the Bible, in the Eucharist, and in everyone you meet. Be His witness to the world!

FOOD FOR THOUGHT

Who has God put on your heart to share His message with? Start praying for that person (or those people) right now, and ask the Holy Spirit for opportunities to share your faith with them, by word and deed. And tomorrow, start reading one of the other three Gospels and continue to draw closer to Jesus Christ, your God.

What's next?

Okay, so you've worked all the way through St. Mark's Gospel, page by page. The story is still fresh in your mind, the glory of the Resurrection resounding in your heart, and the dust of Israel's roads still caked on your flip-flops.

Well done! You've accomplished something amazing when you pray through an entire Gospel. So here's the question...

Now what?

What's next? Where does one go from here? Do you head back to the "beginning" of the story in Genesis? Perhaps move on to one of St. Paul's letters? What's the best way to keep moving forward with praying the Scriptures?

Since the stories and characters are still fresh in your mind, why not try another Gospel. You'll notice similarities but also differences. You'll encounter new stories and emphases, too. When we read the Gospels, it's like reading four versions of one truth... they're like four sides of the same coin (if a coin had four sides, that is).

On the next couple of pages, we're going to give you a brief overview of the other three Gospels and the saints who the Holy Spirit inspired to write them. Why not take some time and work through one or all of the remaining Gospels before moving on to other books in the Bible. You've got your whole life to read and pray God's book.

Spend a little more time immersing yourself in Christ's words and watch as you grow even more deeply in love with God.

Who Are These Other Guys?
An overview of the three "other" Gospel writers.

MATTHEW

Author Background:
- One of the Twelve Apostles
- Originally called Levi, a tax collector (Matthew 10, Luke 5), and a direct eyewitness to Jesus' daily, earthly ministry.

Central Theme of Matthew's Gospel
Christ is the <u>Messiah</u> and <u>King</u> who came to establish a Church.

Audience
Written for Jewish converts to Christianity.

Date
Written (most likely) between the years of 60-65 A.D.

Key Goals of St. Matthew's Gospel
1. *Try to prove (with clear and compelling evidence) that Jesus of Nazareth was the promised <u>Messiah</u>.*
   - … that in Him the ancient prophesies (what was promised in the Old Testament) were fulfilled (completed/ made whole) by Jesus' coming.
   - Matthew shows this connection most clearly by:
     - Connecting Jesus to David and to Abraham
     - Quoting & referencing the Old Testament (over 100 times)
     - Giving John the Baptist (the Prophet who announced Jesus as Messiah) a prominent role in his Gospel

2. *Try to help readers understand Jesus Christ as <u>King</u>.*
   - The leading characteristic of this Gospel is that it puts Christ in a place of glory. Matthew achieves this by:
     - Showing Christ as true heir to David's throne.
     - Using the expression "kingdom of heaven" 32 times.
     - Using references to the King/Kingdom. (The Kingdom is a spiritual one, not a political one.)

3. To provide an early Church "manual" for instruction and administration.

- Through specific stories of Christ's life, Matthew tells his readers that...
    - Jesus' kingdom is nothing like the kingdoms of earth; His kingdom is full of mercy, justice, equality, wisdom, love, and hope.
    - Jesus presents a VISIBLE institution, headed by visible men. Just like the Church is spiritual and visible (not political) — so are we, spiritual (our soul) but still visible.
    - The Church's message is authored by God, not by humans. The Church hands on the faith, She doesn't edit it, only interprets it.

Important Passage from the Gospel of Matthew
Sermon on the Mount –

The best known and least obeyed of anything Jesus said

1. Put your trust in God – Matthew 5:3
2. Repent of your sins – Matthew 5:4
3. Learn gentleness – Matthew 5:5
4. Become righteous – Matthew 5:6
5. Show mercy – Matthew 5:7
6. Grow in holiness – Matthew 5:8
7. Make peace – Matthew 5:9
8. Rejoice through persecution – Matthew 5:10-12

LUKE

Author background
- Luke was probably Greek by birth and a Gentile (non-Christian) convert to Christianity (Colossians 4:10-11).
- He was a doctor by profession.
- He was a traveling companion to Paul for at least a while (you can see this in Philemon 1:24, 2 Timothy 4:11, Colossians 4:14).

Central Theme of Luke's Gospel
Jesus brings <u>liberation</u> and <u>healing</u>.
- Social, political and economic *liberation*
- *Healing* of our sinfulness, faults, and shortcomings

Audience
Written for all non-Jewish readers, but especially Greeks with little knowledge of the Jewish faith.

Date
Written (most likely) between the years of 80-90 A.D.

Key Goals of St. Luke's Gospel
- Emphasizes *compassion* and *feelings* – a very HUMAN Jesus
  - Compassion for the poor, needy, sick, helpless
    - Luke 6:20; 7:37,47; 8:2; 10:33; 15:1; 16:20-21; 17:12; 23:39,43
    - Just like Mary and Joseph were

- Emphasizes grace and salvation
  - The love and forgiveness of Christ are available to all
  - No one was rejected or ignored; Jesus embraced all people with the same grace.

- Emphasizes the Holy Spirit (fourteen times)
  - Luke 1:35,41; 2:25-27; 4:1,14,18; 10:21; 11:13; 24:49

- Emphasizes Mary and the importance of women
  - Luke 7:11-17; 36-50; 8:2-3; 10:38-42

- Emphasizes prayer
  - At Baptism – Luke 3:21
  - In the wilderness – Luke 5:16
  - When choosing His disciples – Luke 6:12
  - At the Transfiguration – Luke 9:29
  - Teaching the Lord's prayer – Luke 11:1
  - Talking to Peter – Luke 22:32
  - At Gethsemane – Luke 22:44
  - At the Cross – Luke 23:46

- Emphasizes humility and the need to leave worldliness and riches behind

- Emphasizes God's glory above our own

- Emphasizes living the Gospel DAILY
  - Luke 9:23; 11:3; 16:19; 19:47; 21:34

JOHN

Author background
- Believed to have written the final Gospel, as well as of the three letters (which bear his name) and the Book of Revelation.
- The younger brother of James, and the son of Zebedee
- The fisherman partner of Peter and sometimes known as one of the "Sons of Thunder" (Mark 3:17).
- He is called the "Beloved Disciple" who was entrusted with Mary's care at the Cross.
- Most likely the youngest of the apostles, and lived the longest of all the Twelve.

Note: Some scholars have at certain points in history tried to say it was not John who wrote the fourth Gospel, but the case for it being John has always been too strong. His case is strong for several reasons, the strongest reason being that the writing of the Gospel has extraordinary detail that had to be from an eyewitness account... detail such as Hebrew traditions, culture, customs, and geography, as well as an attention to numbers (John 2:6; 6:13; 6:19; 21:8; 21:11) and names (John 1:45; 3:1; 11:1; 18:10).

Central Theme of John's Gospel
The identity of Jesus
- John wasn't interested in adding just another biography about Jesus to the other three Gospels in existence. Instead, John wants to show:
    1. Jesus of Nazareth is the *Son of God*
    2. That belief in this Jesus will bring us *life,* eternal life
    3. That eternal life is a whole new kind, a SACRAMENTAL kind.

Audience
Written for the Early Church (close to the end of the First Century), and to a more universal audience than the other Gospels.

Date
Written (most likely) around 90-95 A.D.

Key Goals of St. John's Gospel
- To answer _why_ Jesus came
  - John 20:31 sums it up pretty well

- To answer _who_ Jesus is
  - St. John names Jesus as God
  - Person of Christ in John
  - He utters in John 8:58... "I AM" ...the divine, unutterable name of God (Exodus 3:14).

- John arranges Jesus' words into seven "I AM" statements that reveal His identity
  - "I am the bread of life" (John 6:35)
  - "I am the light of the world" (John 8:12)
  - "I am the gate" (John 10:7)
  - "I am the good shepherd" (John 10:11)
  - "I am the resurrection and the life" (John 11:25)
  - "I am the way and the truth and the life" (John 14:6)
  - "I am the true vine" (John 15:1)

- To answer _what_ Jesus does
  - Jesus is the Miracle Worker

John achieves these goals by arranging his Gospel topically, not chronologically.

www.LifeTeen.com